Ghost-hunting
in the
Yorkshire Dales

Other books
by the same author...
HAUNTED YORKSHIRE
THE CHANGING DALES
LETTERS FROM THE DALES
HIGH DALE COUNTRY

GHOST-HUNTING
IN THE
YORKSHIRE DALES

W R MITCHELL

CASTLEBERG
1996

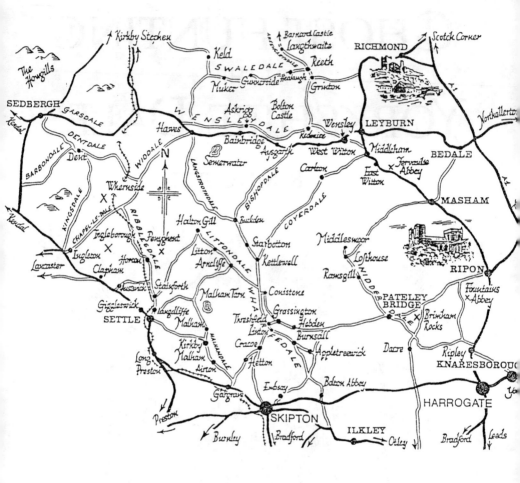

A **Castleberg** Book.

First published in the United Kingdom in 1996.

Copyright © W R Mitchell 1996.

The moral right of the author has been asserted.

ISBN 1 871064 84 8

Typeset in Palacio, printed and bound in the United Kingdom by
Lamberts Printers, Station Road, Settle, North Yorkshire, BD24 9AA.

Published by Castleberg, 18 Yealand Avenue, Giggleswick, Settle,
North Yorkshire, BD24 0AY.

Bolton Priory, Wharfedale

Contents

Illustrations

Front cover, title page and page 92 by Ionicus. Other drawings by Stanley Bond, Peter Fox, E Gower, E Jeffrey, Fred Lawson, Guy Ragland Phillip and Alec Wright. Back cover photograph by the author.

Ordnance Survey

Indispensible companions to this book are three of the Ordnance Survey Outdoor Leisure Maps, 2½" to 1 mile (4cm to 1km)—No 2, Yorkshire Dales (Whernside); No 10—Yorkshire Dales (Malham) and No 30—Yorkshire Dales (Wensleydale).

Spooky Destinations

Ghost-Hunting in the Yorkshire Dales is a cross between a guide and a ghost book. Pick a ghost story which takes your fancy—and, using the instructions, go forth to the place where the ghostly happening occurred. If, of course, there is public access. A ghost-hunter must respect private property or land and be content to look at it from a road or footpath.

Go in search of a spectral hound in Trollers Gill. You may easily distinguish it from a sheep because it is big, hairy and has eyes as big as saucers. Go to Easegill, near Cowan Bridge, and walk on to Bull Pot in the hope of finding witches roosting on the big old trees shading a rent in the limestone. It is encouraging to find a besom propped against a drystone wall.

Organise an expedition from the car park at Malham to Janet's Foss, a fan-shaped waterfall in a mossy gill, and locate the stubby cave used by Jennet, Queen of the Fairies. Or seek the Green Man at Fountains Abbey, standing just outside the Chapel of Nine Altars with the smugness of the only one that day to spot the Green Man, represented by a carving high on an arch. He's ugly. Oak branches (or could they be vines?) extend from his mouth. Satisfy your curiosity about the gentle ghost of Hubberholme Church—the fair-haired woman wearing a blue dress, wife of a former vicar, who occasionally sits in the front pew.

If, at the end, you still do not believe in ghosts—if there has been no sudden chilling of the air, a musty smell nor the clanking of chains—rejoice that you have at least poked your nose into some of the most interesting nooks in the region.

The Yorkshire Dales have a common geological origin but, beyond the fundamentals of the rock layers belonging to the Carboniferous period, no two dales are alike. The old river valleys were the playground of glaciers, which widened, deepened and smoothed the slopes with a geological mush we call boulder clay.

The primeval forest was in tatters several thousand years ago, as Man made his mark on the landscape, and there's not a square yard of true wilderness, but the Dales landscape, with its clear-cut valleys and bare sheep ridges, its limestone pavements and vast tracts of heather moors, with its becks, arched bridges and stone villages, has an alluring quality.

Dales life evolved in isolation. In the upper valleys were the stern, taciturn folk of Norse stock, attending their tups and yows in a succession of solitudes. Until the transport revolution and tourism opened them, the Dales were little known. A tourist of the Romantic Age, collecting a guide, went to places like Gordale Scar in Malhamdale with the wonderment of someone who today explores the headwaters of the Amazon.

The word "dale" is derived from the Norse and means a valley. Each of the major dales has attendant smaller dales and gills, which are water-carved ravines. Swaledale, small and homely, cherishes its classic layout of walls and field barns. Wensleydale, broad and green, has tabular hills and splendid waterfalls. Wharfedale has a gentle nature, with a lime-rich river and fellsides decked with 'hanging' woods.

Malhamdale, the cradle of the Aire, has a stupendous headpiece in the 250ft natural limestone cliff called Malham Cove. The Ribble, flowing westwards, starts in a wild setting, a basin-like area where several small valleys meet under the blue gaze of the Three Peaks, and has its youthful fling down to Settle, whence it progresses in a series of giant ox-bows towards Lancashire.

Charlotte Bronte wrote: "Speak of the North! A lonely moor, silent and still and trackless lies." Anyone who has trudged across the moors which lie between the well-known valleys of the Yorkshire Dales National Park, while appreciating Charlotte's poetic vision, will become aware that the uplands are neither silent nor trackless.

Those with imagination may find their pulses quickening at a sudden awareness of "beings" who lived in these parts down the long years.

Shhh! What's that?

Dales life evolved in isolation, which bred a sturdy resourceful people. Dalehead villages and farms were virtually self-sufficient. The way of life was distinctive, based on pastoral farming. It was a life tuned to the thin soils, a fickle climate and a long, long winter. In good times the people rejoiced. In times of privation they went into partial hibernation and waited for things to improve. And if something went wrong, they could always blame the local witch, ghost, boggart, hob or fairy.

Alf Wight, a vet best known under his pen-name James Herriot, began his association with the Dales in 1940. He told me that when he toured the dalehead farms, he found people treating their stock as best they knew and in a way he could only describe as black magic. The Dalesfolk knew much about upland cattle and sheep but in matters of animal ill-health were often struggling against ailments they only dimly understood.

Rowan warded off witches. A stone with a hole was hung up as a charm. When cows aborted their calves, there was no knowledge of the disease which caused it. Someone tied up a goat in the shippon to help keep the cattle calm. The trouble cleared up. Soon it was the standard remedy. The goat got the credit for alleviating a complaint which normally did not recur in the same stock.

In earlier times, the lives of the Pennine folk were in part ruled by superstition and omens. Strange noises were easily explained. At Camhouses, near the headwaters of the Wharfe, lived a noisy ghost called T'Joiner. One of the Beresford family told a visitor it was because he used to "hammer and bray" all night. He made enough noise to "wakken t'deead". No one seems to have looked for natural causes.

There used to be a grim type of humour. At Cosh, possibly the remotest farm, being situated in a moorland wilderness between the head of Ribblesdale and that of Littondale, there was a "gurt fall o' snow" about Christmastime. Snow hung about until April. When a caller inquired about some sheep, the farmer's wife said her husband died at Christmas. She'd have to do something about getting him buried when the thaw came. The startled caller said: "He'll have gone bad." She replied: "Nay—Ah salted him down. He's aw reight. Come and have a look at him!"

For a cock to crow in a doorway, or a flake of soot to drop from the bars of the fire-grate, you could be sure that a stranger was due. A horseshoe was hung up for luck, but you must be sure to place it with the opening upwards otherwise any good luck would spill out.

What was called a "witch stone" (the stone already mentioned as warding off ill-luck) was known in the Grassington area of Wharfedale as Bitch Daughter Stone, being suspended in stables and cowhouses to guard the stock against witch-borne diseases. To charm away warts, a dalesman gathered smooth pebbles from the river, rubbing each wart with them. The pebbles were then parcelled up and surreptitiously thrown over his head as he stood at four lane ends. If he (or she) did not look back, the warts would vanish.

A Haunted Region

Halliwell Sutcliffe, in *The Striding Dales,* wrote: ''From ancient times the fairies have been with them, the brown men who lurk among the heather spaces, the trolls that haunt deep ravines where the streams go on silent feet, afraid lest any noise of theirs should rouse the spirits.'' Most modern writers about the Dales ignore the famous old ghost stories, many of which are a product of lively Victorian minds but each now adding a little something to the Dales Experience.

Halliwell Sutcliffe, whose imagination worked overtime, wrote: ''There's not a moor-road, or a field path, but is beset by its own haunting. Men and women have travelled these ways since the Dales were young—travelled through centuries that would be forgotten if a ghost did not rise at the right hand or the left to remind one of things unforgettable.''

Most of the ghosts wear old-time garb, the sort which was worn in the seventeenth century or in Victorian times, when ghost stories were especially popular. When the Settle-Carlisle railway cut like a swathe through the high dale country, men were on duty in remote places, such as signal boxes. As the long Pennine winter set in, with winds howling like demons, or snow muffling the sound of a human footfall, the slightest creak could make the sensitive signalman's hair rise on the back of his head.

The agony was prolonged if there was chain-rattling, though a rational explanation was usually forthcoming. Dick Clarke, who for many years served in the signal box at Helwith Bridge, was startled by the sound of a chain. When he plucked up courage to wander out of the box, he found it was a collie dog that had broken away from its kennel. The chain had caught between two capstones as it leapt a wall and the dog was striving vigorously to free itself.

Dick Fawcett told me of the ghost which always walked with its back to the trains. Dick, a railwayman, acknowledged this to be a dangerous pastime—even for a ghost. "He was never seen to walk on the 'down' line. How he got back to his starting point, I wouldn't know."

In wartime, when not a glimmer of artificial light was allow-ed, Dick left his signal box with his shotgun on seeing spec-tral forms against the sky. The strange beings were members of the local Home Guard. In the same period, men guarding Ribblehead viaduct in dark or misty conditions were known to challenge a horse or to equate the rustling of a sheep with a German parachutist. It was only a short step from this state of mental alert to ghost-spotting.

Fairies are back in fashion. Specialist shops are being open-ed at which you might buy stick-on wings, fairy dust and books galore. A London toy shop is reported to be "selling fairies like hot cakes". At the time of writing, several films featuring the gossamer-winged sub-species of fairy are in prospect.

One of the films concerns a cluster of wee folk photographed by two imaginative little girls living at Cottingley, in the Aire Valley, in 1917. A photograph of a girl with a bevy of fairies putting on an air display duped Sir Arthur Conan Doyle, the creator of Sherlock Holmes, who had turned spiritualist and had a touching belief in "wee folk". Doyle, who himself had Yorkshire connections, did not stop to question why these fairies should be clad in the latest Paris fashions.

I met a man who equated Robin Hood, the darling of Hollywood film directors, not with a medieval outlaw clad in Lincoln Green but with an ancient forest fairy. He pointed out some of the obscure places in our northern dale country which have Robin Hood Wells. One of them is to be found on Horse Head Moor, between Littondale and Langstrothdale.

Ghost-hunting in the Yorkshire Dales is not a serious study of the supernatural but a guide to mysterious places for the inquisitive holidaymaker who uses a car and does not mind completing the last few miles of a journey on foot. Most of the ''presences'' mentioned have been well-documented. Some have become part of the tourist industry. Or have been adopted by the entertainment industry, with bizarre settings and with weird music to set our nerves on edge.

There is plenty of scope for updating our ghosts. The hob, a domestic form of fairy, was found at Sturfitt Hall, near Reeth. The owner provided him with a new suit of clothes as a hint he might go and live elsewhere. On a modern television film, he might be clad as a spaceman and sent on his way to wreak havoc on some distant planet.

At the Dales farms, any ghostly wailing or rattling of chains is now drowned out by the roar of tractors or the hidious whine of low-flying aircraft. Gone is the old-time hush, when you might listen to the sound of insects—or the murmuration of ghosts.

A winter night really was dark, with no glare from sodium lighting in the nearest town. We saw just the faint gleam of storm lanterns being used by farmers going about their evening tasks. There were shadows then. And goodness knows what or who was to be found in the dark places.

13

Swaledale

T'Auld Man

Look for T'Auld Man in Gunnerside Gill or at Old Gang, on the northern side of Swaledale, where is to be found the biggest concentration of old mine workings in the Dales. Walkers on Mr Wainwright's Coast to Coast cross the top of the Gill. They continue eastwards over a blighted hilltop to where stands the remains of the Old Gang complex. If you arrive by car, park it either at Gunnerside (where space is limited) or, using the high road between Low Row and Arkengarthdale, at Surrender Bridge.

THE PATH up the gill from Gunnerside passes the remains of Sir Francis Mine to a scattering of ruined structures, including smelt mill and peat store where the path bifurcates. You may return on a higher level, via Bunton Hush, where you can (safely) look into a good example of a mine entrance. If Surrender Bridge is selected, for Old Gang, cross the road and follow a path for a mile or so. The smelt mill chimney is a conspicuous feature. Then (taking care) climb to the moor-edge to see what remains of a unique peat store, which was thatched by ling. Return by the same route.

T'Auld Man is not, strictly speaking, a ghost but a collective term for generations of miners. When anyone spoke of T'Auld Man, it was usually with a mixture of respect and irritation. Having followed up some promising signs of a lead vein he might suddenly break through to an area which had already been worked. T'Auld Man had been there before him.

It is unwise to venture into an old lead mine, where the wood has the puss of decay and a skimming of mud might conceal some rotten boarding, beneath which is a hundred foot shaft. Be content to peep into the mouth of an adit or level, where you may sample the atmosphere.

Here, fringed by spleenworts, is a well masoned arch. Worn sleepers relate to a subterranean tramway on which the traffic was tubs, hauled by ponies. Water drips into pools with a sound which is weirdly amplified by the close conditions. T'Auld Man is there—but he doesn't make a song and dance about it.

Swaledale bears the scars of lead mining. The fellsides are scored deeply at a hush, where water was dammed, then suddenly released to expose the mineral veins. Spoil heaps testify to the incredible energy of T'Auld Man.

Crumbling bouse-bays, compartments made of dry stone and situated near the mouth of a mine, housed galena (lead ore) before it began the process leading to ingots of lead. Collapsed flues lead the eyes to where chimneys stand on hilltops with the visual emphasis of exclamation marks. The last big mines were closed in the 1870s and 1880s, a time when much cheaper lead was being imported from Spain.

What of the miners who collectively represent T'Man in Dales folklore? The Swaledale lead miner, who was referred to as a gruver, had a chancy occupation. He and friends usually formed a partnership and negotiated with the mine agent to work a certain area, drawing their income from what they mined.

The typical Swaledale miner had a large family living on a small-holding and while he was in the mine his wife attended to the stock. He would take time off for the haymaking. His work a short life and not a particularly merry one. If he had sons, he took them to the mine to help him in his work. An eight-year-old lad who started work holding candles for miners later took turns operating the ''windy king'', which was designed to send a current of air into the workings. While still in his thirties, the miner might succumb to the dreaded gruver's complaint, which was a combination of silicosis and gas poisoning.

Below ground, the air reverberated to the clang of the heavy hammer against a hand-held drill as holes were made for explosives. The work was done by the light of a tallow candle, bedded on clay and stuck on any ledge on the wall of the mine. The crump of explosions, first with gunpowder, then with gelignite, led to stale and dusty air.

A tapping sound in a Swaledale lead mine, ascribed to T'Auld Man, was welcome, indicating to the superstitious miners that a good vein was in the offing. Conditions in a mine were too grim even for ghosts. Among the surface screes in the Gunnerside area have been found traces of Early Man. When John Cherry was "ferreting" among stones at the base of a cliff, he located a human skeleton, which turned out to be that of a young man buried in a sitting position, with stone flags round about. John returned to the place with

Muker, Swaledale.

his friend Talbot Raw. As they worked to free the skeleton, Tal observed: "Nivver mind botherin' wi' them bones. Look for 'is purse.''

Visit the Folk Museum at Reeth for a general introduction to lead-mining. Then motor to Low Row (Swaledale) or turn left just beyond Langthwaite (Arkengarthdale) to follow a high road popularised by the BBC in their introduction to the James Herriot series. Near Surrender Bridge, there is off-road parking.

Follow the wide track westwards to Old Gang, where a smelt mill chimney and ruined buildings stand amid an area desecrated by T'Auld Man. On the moor-edge are the remains of a unique peat store, now represented by two rows of stone pillars and gable ends which indicates by their steepness that it was once thatched, possibly with ling.

Lead-mining country is patterned by miners' trods, walkways which were habitually followed by the men. Now and again, while on their way to work, a group of miners would stop for a smoke, squatting on their heels to inhale black twist through clay pipes and meanwhile yarning—about the mines. They had few other topics but their work. Even at home, with some friends, a man would trace on the floor the layout of some workings, specifying on future prospects.

T'Auld Man was superstitious. Luck-stones, which had holes in the middle and were threaded with string, have been found in places where he worked. The lead-miner did not want to tempt fate. When the mines closed; many families emigrated to the industrialised areas of County Durham or East Lancashire. Bob Carter recalled for me a day in 1902 when a traction engine with two trucks in tow moved down the dale. It was taking tramlines from the now disused mines to Richmond station for transportation to a scrapyard.

The mines were left in the custody of T'Auld Man.

Swinnergill Kirk

Approach from Keld, following the Coast to Coast route high above the Swale and with the blocky form of Kisdon, the "island hill" beyond. Pass a ruined building, which was formerly Crackpot Farm, and follow the path round to where the remains of a smelt mill lie near a packhorse-type bridge over the stream. Swinnergill Kirk lies up the ravine. Take great care when visiting it, for the stones are invariably slippery.

WHEN AND WHY the name Swinnergill Kirk was given to a mossy cave at the head of a lile ravine is not known. Theories abound. One, which was recounted by R Wilfrid Crosland, the Quaker historian of Yorkshire ways, was that the parson of Muker in 1662 was a Nonconformist and went into the wilderness with the other 2,000 Nonconforming clergy (not to the same place, I hasten to add).

The Muker man's congregation stood by him, hid him and housed him and held their services regularly in the Kirk until freedom to worship was established by law in 1689. Meanwhile, the Confirming Vicar appointed to Muker had carried on with a much depleted congregation.

My favourite route to Swinnergill is along a high track which branches off from the byroad west of Gunnerside Lodge. In spring, lapwings wail a warning to their young, which snuggle into the reed beds and keep their heads down. Where old walls and grey screes are plentiful, the "stean chat" (wheatear) moves in its typical jerky manner and punctuates a still day with its whistles and chacking. In Swinnergill itself, you should hear the fluty voice of the ring ouzel, our north-country nightingale.

Where the ground has been disturbed by mining, the white, star-like flowers of spring sandwort brighten the dull ground, this plant being one of the few to be tolerant of lead. In places, the sandwort is massed like daisies on a lawn.

At Swinnergill, the eye is captured by the bridge, which is finely masoned, springing from cliff to cliff across the rocky bed of the stream. The first smelt mill to be built hereabouts was in the eighteenth century, when Lord Pomfret held the mining rights.

Years ago, when I walked to Swinnergill with Matthew Cherry, he showed me a fireplace—an incongruous feature now, set in a fragment of building and open to all the winds that blow. Matthew's family surname was among a small number carved on the stone surround. We heard the crowing of a pheasant, and I heard that when this species was introduced to Upper Swaledale it was known to the locals as "that long-tailed bird". Some pheasants were killed and stuffed, to be proudly exhibited in local homes.

Beyond the bridge, the cliffs close in and a visitor looks through a dark curtain of rowan leaves. The scolding voice of a wren is especially loud in the echo-chamber between the grey cliffs. The visitor negotiates the edges of pools to reach a moss cliff over which falling water has gone white with fury.

In times of spate (when you should stay out of this stretch of Swinnergill), tumbling water and its spray hide the 70ft long cave in which early Nonconformists are said to have worshipped in those old-time days of religious intolerance. It is said that crude pictures and scriptural texts were traced on the walls.

The story is vague in folk memory and unsubstantiated by any document. Was it true, as Matthew Cherry had heard, that when services were being held at this secluded place, scouts were stationed on the hills round about to keep a watch for strangers? Might the group of worshippers have been Catholics, who at one time had to worship surreptitiously for fear of being arrested? Was there once a large block of stone here which served as an altar?

Swinnergill's cave was used as a refuge after a skirmish

between a party of Scotsmen and Dalesmen during the Jacobite Rebellion of 1745. There was a tradition that after defeat in the '45, two brothers, James and George Birkbeck, wandered into Swaledale and, settling at Melbecks, planted two Scots pines as a sign that if any supporters of the Stuart cause were in need, they would be secretly and hospitably received at "the sign of the firs".

Once, in this district, I heard what sounded like maniacal laughter. It turned out to be a round of alarm calls by a peregrine falcon.

The Corpse Road

Park the car at Muker and walk through the village to gain the path leading on to Kisdon Hill. This was a high stretch of the route taken by bearers and mourners at dalehead funerals when the nearest consecrated ground was at Grinton, where a kirk stood in Norman times and grew mightily in the Middle Ages, the old parish extending to no less than 50,000 acres. The need for a Corpse Road ended in 1580, when a church was built at Muker. A so-called coffin-stone at Ivelet Bridge, west of Gunnerside, is more likely to be part of the bridge abutment. The lane leading to the bridge is said to be haunted. A black dog, gliding silently on to the bridge and disappearing over the ledge, is seen as a portend of a tragic event.

SWALEDALE has the best-known of several Corpse Roads. And, of course, they were not just used for the transportation of the dead to consecrated ground. If you are imaginative, you might like to find a stone to sit on and half close your eyes as you ponder on wayfaring down the years, from the prehistoric hunting parties, some of whom lost flint arrowheads which were picked up and studied in recent times.

Packhorses, laden with salt, corn, cloth or panniers of lead, passed along the old route, which lay well above the boggy ground of the dale floor. Pedlars and packmen, "badgers" and "higglers" went from farm to farm. The farmers themselves and clerics would help to make up a company as diverse and interesting in its way as the famous Canterbury pilgrims.

A funeral procession consisted of the bearers of the "dear departed" who in those early times was conveyed in a wicker basket. The mourners shuffled along behind. They used a route on the sunny side of Swaledale, over Kisdon Hill, between Keld and Muker, then forded the Swale to contour on Iveletside, on the northern side of the dale.

The unburied dead were carried along various tracks, depending whether the deaths had occured. If anyone died at West Stonesdale or Ravenseat, the funeral party would keep to the left bank of the Swale and join the Corpse Way at Calvert Houses. Use was made of traditional waths or fords, as was most convenient. In days before there were bridges in the upper dale, a decision about which route to use would depend largely on the state of the river. In any case, a pony would be used to bear the coffin across the water.

Relatives of the dead person had kept watch over the body in turn. Relatives and neighbours were "bidden" to the funeral by personal calls. The dale families were huge and as many as two hundred people might thus be informed of the death and of the funeral arrangements. A funeral could be a drain on the family resources, especially if it extended into a second day, because it was customary for guests to live at the expense of the bereaved.

On the funeral day, special biscuits and wine were handed over the coffin to the guests as they turned up at the house. The first team of bearers hoisted the wicker-coffin on to their shoulders for the journey to Grinton. They were able to rest at intervals. In the old days, Shoregill Head, near Ivelet, was probably a farm-cum-inn, and Calvert Houses had a beer tavern known as The Traveller's Rest.

Above Feetham are the foundations of a wayside mortuary,

referred to as the "dead-house". Here the coffins might be safely left while the funeral party went to the Punch Bowl for liquid refreshment. Dalesfolk used to tell of the day when two funeral parties used the mortuary simultaneously, and both were more than adequately "refreshed" at the inn. In their befuddled state, each party picked up the other's coffin. Only after the interment (when, presumably, the men had sobered up) was the mistake discovered.

Edmund Cooper, historian of Swaledale, recorded that if the dead man was a shepherd, a fleece of wool was placed in the coffin to explain his absence from Church on several occasions. He had been attending to his flock and was not dealt with too harshly on the Day of Judgement.

Wicker-coffins were in use until the early part of the eighteenth century, for in 1716 the curate of Muker announced that he would bury no more corpses without coffins. In 1836, Muker acquired a horse-drawn hearse, a box-like structure on four wheels, each of which was lined with leather to deaden the sound.

A fee of sixpence was charged for its use by local families. Outsiders were charged at the rate of sixpence a mile. It was the custom to stop the cortege at the school, where the coffin was hauled out through the back of the hearse and lifted on the shoulders of the pall-bearers. During the procession, the mourners chanted a solemn dirge.

When the mother of Richard Kearton, the pioneer wildlife photographer, died at Nateby, arrangements had been made for her to be buried at Muker but on the night before the funeral was to take place, a blizzard struck the area. Richard, keen that his mother's wishes should be carried out to the letter, employed a team of men to cut a way to Muker. The coffin was transported on a horse-drawn sled.

King Arthur at Richmond

Richmond-by-the-Swale, on the A6108, which extends
from Scotch Corner (A1) to Ripon, is a perfect castle-town,
one of the most fascinating in England. This was the *riche
mont* (strong hill) of the Norman lords and construction of
the castle, with its 100ft keep, was started by Rufus the Red
just five years after the Conquest.

BY ALL MEANS visit the Castle and climb the steps to the
top of the keep, but the story of Potter Thompson goes back
to the time of King Arthur, which is before William the Con-
queror and his knights began to throw their weight about.
Arthur and *his* knights were thorns in the flesh of the in-
vading Angles round about the year AD500.

Potter Thompson, in a much-told story, went to the river
bank to escape his wife's nagging tongue. Or was it to get
some clay for his potter's wheel? He saw an opening in the
rock beneath the castle. He entered and found himself in a
passage leading to a huge cavern. Let us allow Arthur H Nor-
way (*Highways and Byways in Yorkshire*, 1899) give an account of what happened:

'' . . . a lofty cavern stretched away so far on either hand that
even the bright light of the lamp hanging in an old cresset
from the ceiling could not scatter the thick shadows nor
reveal the limits of the cavern. Underneath the lamp there
stood a stone table, on which were laid a gigantic horn—such
a horn as Potter Thompson had never seen before, rich and
wonderful with gold and ivory.

''Now this was what Potter saw in the first moment; in the
next he distinguished huge figures of knights in armour lying
asleep on the floor of the cavern, and among them one who
bore on his helmet a crown of gold, and lay breathing gently
in his slumber as if he dreamt of none but sweet and pleasant
things.

''So Potter Thompson, the poor fool, stood and held his

breath and watched them, while his heart beat heavily and his scared wits told him he was looking on a sight that never living man had seen before. There lay King Arthur and his knights sleeping, as he had known they would be found, waiting for the hour when England called for them.

"And as he watched that strange and noble sight, the desire grew eager in him to carry off some proof that he had indeed beheld it; and he stole on tiptoe to the table, and laid hand upon the sword and horn and lifted them, and was stealing back towards the gloomy passage which had brought him thither when the dark vault rang with a clash of steel and a knight turned over in his sleep and raised himself upon his arm, and fear seized on Potter Thompson and he dropped the horn and sword and fled.

Richmond, Swaledale

"But as he went, a loud voice mocked him, crying at his back:

Potter, Potter Thompson!
If thou hads't either drawn
The sword, or blown the horn,
Thou'ds't been the luckiest man
That ever yet was born.

"So Potter Thompson went, and lost his fortune because his heart failed him. Rarely does a second chance come to a man who cannot grasp the first, and Potter never found again the winding passage which had led him into the bowels of the mountain."

Just as colourful is the tale of the little Drummer Boy who was sent by soldiers along a long, dark tunnel which was said to extend from Richmond Castle to Easby Abbey. Away he went, playing boldly on his drum. The soldiers, listening to the muffled sound, followed the course through the streets of the town. The sound of the drum became fainter and fainter and, when the men arrived at the spot now occupied by Richmond Grammar School, it stopped altogether.

The little drummer boy was not seen again. The beat of his drum might be heard, faint and distant, on quiet days.

Wensleydale

Macfie of Lunds

From The Moorcock Inn, at the head of Wensleydale, the B6259 has the company of the Settle-Carlisle Railway. Park near the former railway cottages at Aisgill, by the highest stretch of the famous line and you might cross the railway by a substantial bridge and follow a track passing near a splendid waterfall which is fed by water from Hell Gill, the cradle of the River Eden. The Ure, river of Wensleydale, begins with a gathering of runnels on the fellside ahead. For Lunds Church, use a footpath from The Quarry (consult your Ordnance map) and make your way for a quarter of a mile through a tract of conifers and across the beck.

LUNDS CHURCH, which looks from a distance like a small barn, was established about 1600 as a chapel-of-ease in the vast parish of Aysgarth. The building is surrounded by a large graveyard where some of the commemorative stones lie flat, being liberally sprinkled with sheep droppings. To the sheep they are a dry resting places as they rest and chew the cud.

One gravestone marks the last resting place of R A Scott Macfie, a bachelor member of a well-to-do Liverpool family who arrived in the upper Dales just after the 1914-18 war, in which he had served, to spend his later days at Shaws, a converted farmhouse standing well over 1,000ft above sea level. Macfie hoped to develop his little estate and and provide proper access to the church. He made a start on an approach drive, providing splendid gateposts and wrought-ironwork which carried his monogram. Trees were planted in a virtually treeless area.

A large wooden hut was erected at Shaws as a repository for his books, pictures and some furniture. He added two wooden rooms to the old farmhouse, one to be a parlour for a housekeeper and the other a bedroom for himself. He wrote: "It is a rather dangerous walk on dark windy nights from the enlarged cottage to the hut. There is a step of the waterfall actually in the garden, but the main fall is higher up and hidden, and above it is a sort of Hell Gill on a small scale."

He loved company, particuarly that of the local dalesfolk, some of whom shook their heads sadly from time to time at Macfie's more outlandish ideas, though they absorbed several which improved their farming methods. He tried to introduce the Scrub-Bull scheme and studied canine hysteria.

Macfie attended tiny Lunds church "and they don't close the church door until after my (often late) arrival." Impatient of dogma, looking for a religion which was practical, he claimed that Lunds should have a young man as a parson, someone who could play football with the lads after the church on a Sunday.

If there is a ghost at Lunds Church, which incidentally is no longer used for regular worship, it is unlikely to be Macfie, though he was an expert on gypsy lore who allowed his gypsy friends to park on his land. Do the spirits of the "travellers" still range across the countryside they once knew? Or could there be a ghostly procession for the dead of Cotterdale were borne over High Abbotside and down to Lunds Church for burial.

Early this century, the writer Edwin Bogg was shown the grave of Thread Jack, an itinerant pedlar of small wares for womenfolk. Many pedlars came to sad ends, so maybe out there is the uneasy spirit of Thread Jack. Perhaps Auld Deborah endures as a spectral cart-horse. When Macfie died in 1935, his coffin, draped in the Union Jack, was placed on a cart drawn by his horse. Twenty or thirty black-coated dalesmen were in the company of mourners. One of them was heard to say: "Eh, that's auld Deborah. Many's the time he's told me as how he liked her that much that, if she died, he'd put up a tombstone for her. An' now he's gone first."

Lunds is a quiet spot, during the lulls between visits by low-flying RAF aircraft. A Victorian parson's farewell address to his congregation was: "You do not love one another, and God does not love you; for in all these three or four years I have ministered here, there has not been a marriage or a death."

The Whistling Soldier

Go northward from the Moorcock Inn on B6259 and within a short distance you will see across some pastureland (left) a large metal footbridge, which straddles the Settle-Carlisle Railway at Grizedale Crossing. The Ordnance Map indicates a footpath to Grizedale, a remote area populated by a few people, rather more fell ponies and lots of hardy hill sheep. Grizedale achieved fame through a television film entitled *The Dale that Died*. (Rumours of its death were premature!).

ONE OF the worst railway accidents took place between Garsdale and Aisgill on Christmas Eve, 1910, when the St Pancras to Glasgow express ran into two light engines which the signalman at Garsdale, during a stressful shift, had cleared but forgotten about. The distraught man reported to his superiors: "I have wrecked the Scotch express."

Richard Fawcett (a railwayman known widely as Rabbity Dick from his poaching activities) told me of a ghostly whistle heard at night by the denizens of the railway workers' house at Grizedale Crossing. In the early 1930s, Dick worked in and around Hawes Junction (Garsdale) station as a member of the

Slip and Drainage Gang. At mealtimes or on wet days, when the men assembled in one of the lineside huts, he heard them yarning about local matters.

Joe Gamsby, one of the best story-tellers, was a ganger who lived in one of the Grizedale Cottages. Joe's father-in-law, Will Slinger, had been the first ganger on the Lunds Length and the first man to live in one of the railway cottages. Joe and his wife reared a son and six daughters. Joe's son-in-law, who lived in the next house, had a wife who was the crossing keeper. She was not over-worked. As Dick Fawcett told me: "She'd perhaps have to let someone over the crossing twice a year but had to be there, just in case."

The Slinger family were familiar with the Whistle in the Dark. Joe first heard the strange sound on a winter's night when he was courting Bess, one of the Slinger girls. He was sitting in the cottage with her family when the shrill sound was heard outside the building. No one commented on it. Mr Slinger had simply looked up from his newspaper and said: "It's nobbut t'whistle."

It seems that when the Settle-Carlisle was built, there stood at Lunds a ruined cottage, which was cleared when Grizedale Railway Crossing was installed. Under the hearth of the old cottage was found a skeleton; fragments of red tunic clung to it. Metal buttons were also found. The remains indicated that the body had been that of a Scottish soldier.

The story, as passed down, was that he had been courting the daughter of the family who lived in the cottage. The father was annoyed when he found out about the liaison. One night, as the soldier sat on the wall outside and whistled for his girl, father struck him down from behind and he died instantly. After the rest of the family had gone to bed, father buried the soldier's body in the ash-hole, the large square hole under the hearth where ash from the fire fell, to be cleared out annually.

Grannie Slinger told Rabbity Dick that on a moonlit night when there was a hard frost to put a crust on the lying snow, she and her husband had just got into bed and had blown out the candle when they heard the whistle. Looking out of the window, they saw the uniformed soldier seated on the fence in full view of the house.

As Grannie said: "We stared a second or two and he just seemed to fade away." When asked if she had been scared, her reply was: "No, poor lad, he won't harm anybody. He is just wanting his girl friend to join him."

Ghost of Rigg House

Rigg House is set among trees on the high side of the A684 west of Hardraw and not far beyond where a fingerpost marks the way to Cotter Force. One name applies to what are clearly two separate buildings.

ORIGINALLY, one large house stood here. It was owned by a sullen and unpopular man who was nicknamed "Blackwhipper" because he had once owned slaves. His housekeeper, who struggled on despite her advanced age, disappeared mysteriously. Ere long, rumours that a headless spectre had been seen in Rigg House were circulating through the upper dale.

Metcalfe eventually left the district but the hauntings continued. The headless ghost manifested herself in one of the rooms in the central portion, so the owner had that part pulled down, leaving the two ends.

I have also heard it said that the ghostly manifestation was of a coach and four, which followed an old route hereabouts. The middle part of Rigg House was demolished to let the spectral outfit through.

A Queen at Nappa Hall

Nappa Hall, with a medieval plan, is tucked away almost out of sight of travellers on the road which runs north of the river. Nappa is a private house, to which the public is not normally admitted, though bed and breakfast bookings are taken. A footpath (see Ordnance map) passes nearby but the house is screened by outbuildings. The castellated main tower of Nappa can be seen from the nearby road, just east of the hamlet called Nappa Scar.

NAPPA HALL was built between 1450 and 1459. The work was done for Thomas Metcalfe, a warrior who "waxed rich and builded...two faire towers". Nappa's great days were

31

in the sixteenth century. Mary Queen of Scots, a prisoner en route for London, spent six months at Bolton Castle. It is popularly supposed that she was invited to Nappa Hall on at least two occasions and stayed the night.

Her host, Sir Christopher Metcalfe, was High Sheriff of York in 1556. Christopher gloried in his wealth and status. When he met the Judges, he had a following of three hundred mounted attendants. Each was a Metcalfe or related to this illustrous family. And each wore the Metcalfe livery. He married Elizabeth, whose father, Henry Clifford, was the First Earl of Cumberland, of Skipton Castle.

Nappa Hall, Wensleydale

The Queen of the Scots must have liked Nappa Hall, for her spirit is said to haunt the place. In the book *About Yorkshire,* written by Thomas and Katherine Macquoid, and published in 1883, a letter is quoted from a lady who stayed here in 1878. She wrote: ''I was in the hall playing hide-and-seek with the farmer's little girl, a child about four years old. The hall was dimly lighted by a fire and by the light from a candle in a room in the east tower. While at play someone entered the hall from the lower end and walked towards the dais.

''Thinking it was the farmer's wife I ran after her and was going to touch her when she turned round, and I saw her face: it was very lovely. Her dress seemed to be made of black velvet. After looking at me for a moment, she went on and disappeared through the door leading to the winding stone staircase in the angle turret of the west tower. Her face, figure, and general appearance reminded me of portraits of Mary, Queen of Scots.''

At the time of this vision, the bedstead associated with the Queen was still at Nappa Hall.

Ballad of Semerwater

Drive to Bainbridge, on the A684, and travelling directly from the village pass along the edge of Countersett and turn left for a steep descent to the outflow of Semerwater, which laps and frets in a glaciated limestone valley damm- ed by a lateral moraine.The lake is fed by swift and precipitous streams. Raydale Beck is joined by Cragdale Beck, then Marsett Beck and collectively (as Crook Beck) they flow into the lake. In summer, there is the drone of motor boats with water-skiers in train. At other times it might be flooded or frozen.

THE BALLAD of Semerwater, with its tale of a proud city overwhelmed by a flood because of its inhospitality towards a poor stranger, was based on an ancient folk memory. When Sir William Watson presented it in stylish verse, generations of schoolchildren memorised the words.

Watson (a Yorkshireman) richly embroidered an old ac- count of a story passed on from the remote past and Chris- tianised in the process to become yet another medieval morality tale. Then, in 1937, the outflow of the lake was dredged and the normal water level fell by over two feet. Into view came objects—traces of wooden piles, pieces of bone and flint—associated with what the archaeologists of the time considered to have been a lake village, constructed on an artificial island. A fine spearhead was found plastered with clay.

At Semerwater, a flash flood doubles the area of water in an hour or two, with awesome effect. Once or twice in a lifetime water was known to flow over the Carlow Stone, a huge boulder which was ice-borne to its position near the outflow. Two ponderous stones jutting side-by-side from the edge of the lake quite near to the Carlow Stone, have been almost swallowed by alluvial material. They are believed to be part of a single stone. A university party who dug down for eight feet did not reach the base.

Sir William Watson (1858-1935), who gave us an intensely moving *Ballad of Semerwater*, was a native of Burley-in-Wharfedale. His mother hailed from Wensleydale. When the family moved to Liverpool, he enjoyed Dales holidays, during which he carried out research into his Dales forebears, tracing the family back to the fourteenth century. He had hoped to become Poet Laureate but was not selected.

Watson wished his family ties with the Dales to be better known and that wish became true when he wrote what Halliwell Sutcliffe considered to be "the most alluring ballad of our modern times." It concludes:

> *He has cursed aloud that city proud:*
> *He has cursed it in its pride:*
> *He has cursed it into Semerwater*
> *Down the brant hillside.*
> *He has cursed it into Semerwater*
> *There to bide...*
> *King's tower and Queen's bower*
> *And a mickle town and tall:*
> *By glimmer of scale and gleam of fire,*
> *Folk have seen them all.*
> *King's tower and Queen's bower*
> *And weed and reed in the gloom;*
> *And a lost city of Semerwater,*
> *Deep asleep till Doom...*

Burning Old Bartle

Penhill, one of the highspots of Upper Wensleydale, is a fitting backcloth for a 400-year-old whodunnit, a fanciful story perpetuated by local folk, who by and large are down-to-earth. Each August, at the long-drawn-out village of West Witton, the distant past is evoked by the Burning of Bartle.

THE DATE selected is the Saturday nearest to St Bartholomew's Day, which occurs on the 24th. The date may be close to the patronal festival of the Church, but Burning Bartle is no Christian occasion. "We have a procession. The atmosphere is so charged, it's like a pagan rite," said an old lady, unemotionally. "What do they want to go making a fuss of a sheep-stealer for?"

Who was Bartle? His story appears to be pure folklore, with not a scrap of information to satisfy a historian. Through him we may be harking back to prehistory. As related today, the story is of a man caught in the act of taking a sheep. He was pursued from the heights of Penhill to the edge of the village, where he met his end. The precise route is recalled by doggerel verse that is recited on the August night his effigy is borne round the village:

> In Penhill Crags he tore his rags;
> At Hunter's Thorn he blew his horn;
> At Capplebank Stee he brake his knee;
> At Grisgill Beck he brake his neck;
> At Wadsham's End he made his end.
> Shout, lads, shout.

The man who has carried Bartle on his nocturnal rounds for many years told me: "When you're carrying him in a crowd, you feel a bit strange at times. Then you get a drink or two— and you don't bother the same!"

35

Middleham

Woman in Black

Coverdale extends from Middleham (A6108) towards Wharfedale, a descent into which is by the notorious Park Rash. On the moors near Middleham are the training grounds of racehorses. Coverham is the first village to be encountered. Scrafton Moors are above the village of West Scrafton, which is on a loop road, beginning at Coverham and returning to the main route through the dale just beyond Carlton.

PARTICULAR to Coverdale is the story of the Woman in Black. She was an element of a triangular drama involving two lovers. She planned to elope with one of them but the third party murdered the woman. Her body was never found. Years later, some peat-cutters on the Scrafton Moors came across the skeleton of a woman, and beside it was a piece of black cloth and a boot. Surely this was the Woman in Black. A local man who owned a greyhound, trained at Northallerton, named it after the ghost.

This apparition moves under cover of darkness, walking from Coverham church gates to the point on Middleham Moor known as Courting Wall Corner. The Woman in Black wears sombre garb, as though in mourning.

Three women who lived at Tupgill Park, about half a mile above Coverham Church, were driving home from Middleham in a horse and trap when, at the gate leading from the west end of the moor, a female figure wearing black was seen. They asked her to open the gate. She vanished.

A "ghost light", seen on the road between the hamlets of Caldbergh and West Scrafton, takes the form of a brilliant beam which is equally mysteriously switched off when approached. Motorists seeing the light, and coming to a standstill on the narrow country lane to allow what they took to be a vehicle to pass, have waited in vain. Local people connected the "ghost light" with the nearby ruins of St Simon's chapel.

Wharfedale

Haunted Hubberholme

However many people throng the dale, it is quiet and peaceful in Hubberholme Church. Sunlight slants through multi-coloured windows to pick out some of the distinctive features. The Rood Screen is a remnant of medieval times. Robert Thompson, the Kilburn craftsman, made the pews and adorned them with carvings of his trademark, a "church mouse".

A STAINED glass window was fitted in memory of the Falshaw family, who have farmed by the infant Wharfe for centuries. On another window, Pastor Lindley, curate of Halton Gill and Hubberholme, is seen mounted on a white horse as he crosses a snowbound Horse Head Pass to take a service. In the church is a plaque to J B Priestley, writer, who while not being noted for his church-going when alive, regarded Hubberholme as a very special place. (Priestley's ashes, in their urn, were stored for a short time before interment under the stairs at a local farm).

On dull days, the church is gloomy. It adds to the sense of mystery. But generally there are some stray sunbeams to enliven the place. A visitor to Hubberholme at Eastertime some forty years ago was impressed by the serenity and the way the sunlight, streaming through the windows, made patches of light on the flagged floor.

She was with members of her family. The vicar arrived and they chatted with him. She glanced through the central opening of the Rood Screen down the length of the church. In a patch of sunlight towards the right hand side, a figure was sitting. It was a lady with fair hair, parted in the middle and drawn down each side of her face. She wore a blue dress of a style long since gone out of fashion.

The visitor looked away, then returned the glance to find that the mysterious person was sitting quietly in the front pew. The visitor felt a sudden chill. The back of the watcher's neck prickled and a shiver passed down her spine. The Lady in Blue vanished.

On the following Easter, the visitor and her family once again visited Upper Wharfedale and entered Hubberholme Church. They sat in silence for a while. Nothing out of the ordinary was experienced. Then they noticed a stained glass window erected in memory of a vicar's wife who died many years ago. She had fair hair. She was wearing—a blue dress.

I have known several vicars of Hubberholme, including Hugh Hunter, who in 1961, shortly after arriving here, set off with his wife to visit Cam Houses, a remote cluster of farms which lies in the parish of Horton-in-Ribblesdale but so unhandy that the residents were considered to be within the Hubberholme ''sphere of influence''.

They ran into hill mist and left their car some distance short of Cam Houses, continuing the journey on foot. Mrs Hunter being over-tired, the Vicar was glad to see some bales of hay at the side of the road, for it indicated the first farm was not far away. A dark grey dog of what he thought to be the whippet-type emerged from behind the bales, crossed the road in front of the walkers and vanished over the moor. He concluded the dog was taking a short cut home. The dog did not bark nor make a fuss.

The Vicar and his wife reached the farm and thought no more about the dog until, returning home, Mrs Hunter looked up *Yorkshire Tour,* by Ella Pontefract and Marie Hartley, and read about Jerry, a dog which haunts the path from Cam Houses.

Fox with a Shiny Nose

The usual route to the summit of Buckden Pike is from the car park at Buckden, along a well-marked path which crosses National Trust land. Alternatively, park the car (if you can find space) at Starbotton, a few miles lower down the valley, on a footpath (see Ordnance Map) which brings you to the southern end of Buckden Pike—and into the company of the fox with a shiny nose.

CLIMBING from Starbotton, you cross the Peat Ground, where cotton grass, the great peat-forming plant of the Pennines, is thinly spread and yellow mountain pansies shiver in the lightest of breezes. Breaking the Wharfedale skyline, take in the features of the eastern fells, moors and little dales, stretching towards the great Plain of York, beyond which (to be seen in clear conditions) is the grey-blue edge of the North York Moors.

The fox stares unblinkingly, even when a rambler strolls up to it and rubs its nose—for luck. Hence the shine. As you have suspected, the fox is not one of the flesh-and-blood variety. This fox fashioned in metal, being a feature on the memorial to five of the six Polish members of a wartime RAF crew who died when their Wellington bomber crashed in this high and lonely ridge during the 1939-45 war.

The Polish airmen had been on a training flight in January, 1942, a time of year when our Pennine hills are usually crusted by snow and ice. The aircraft brushed the felltop not far from the summit of Buckden Pike and the surviving member of the crew, though badly injured, began a painful, protracted descent of the Pike on all fours.

In this heroic bid to survive, the chances of reaching one of the farms scattered about this high fell country were slight. Then he saw a track in the snow. A fox was preceding him. Where was it going? The airman hoped it was seeking food at a farm or village. Otherwise, if he followed the tracks, he would surely perish on yet another tract of bleak country.

The aviator followed the tracks to the hamlet of Cray, by the Kidstones Pass, where he was able to arouse the Parker family. They attended to his needs. So when a memorial was raised on Buckden Pike, a fox was given a prominent position. Pieces of the Wellington bomber have been concreted into the base of the monument. (The bodies of the victims were interred at Newark).

Secret of Darnbrook Farm

Darnbrook, one of the big old farms of Malham Moor, is now owned by the National Trust. The farm is seen by those crossing from Malham to Arncliffe. A gate across the road inhibits the movement of sheep. Beyond, the road rises steeply, with some sharp bends, then descends equally steeply to Arncliffe, which is in Littondale.

FOR YEARS, a story circulated in Littondale that if you stood in a certain spot near Arncliffe you might hear someone poking the fire at Darnbrook Farm. Then in 1975, workmen at Darnbrook found an extensive underground system, knowledge of which had been lost since Walter Morrison, the Craven millionaire, presided over the Malham Tarn Estate. His name was among those inscribed on the walls of the cave.

It is assumed that as the cave ran underneath the farmhouse, it relayed the sound of someone using a poker on the fire. The cave was named Robinson Pot after the family who farmed it for many years.

Mysterious tapping sounds are not confined to Darnbrook. When the Grassington lead mines were being worked, the miners spoke of The Knockers, supernatural beings living in the mines who warned the men of any accident that was about to occur. In Victorian days, belief in them was absolute. If any noises were heard underground, they were at once attributed to The Knockers. Those who heard the sound feared for their safety and in some cases downed tools and went home.

Water-Babies

Charles Kingsley's The Water-Babies was partly inspired by short visits the author paid to Malham Tarn for the excellent trout fishing. Kingsley, the guest of Walter Morrison at Malham Tarn House, is thought to have introduced his aquatic babies to the cool, clear water of Malham Beck, but Arncliffe, in Littondale, would repay a visit by water baby-spotters. When travelling up Wharfedale, bear left just beyond Kilnsey Crag and you will shortly arrive at Arncliffe, a village where most of the houses huddle around a green. Go to the river bridge and look down on the River Skirfare. If no water-babies are in sight, look instead at Bridge House, which was visited by the celebrated parson-author.

KINGSLEY was for many years Rector of Eversley, in Hampshire, but but he held an honorary position at Middleham in Wensleydale and (as related) he knew Limestone Yorkshire well. You may recall that Tom the Chimney Sweep was taken by his master, Mr Grimes, to Hartover House (Malham Tarn House) and that Tom lost his way in the chimney system and descended into a beautiful room in which a girl was sleeping.

Tom, terrified of what would be said, ran away, descending "Lewthwaite Crag", where he met a woman in a red petticoat as she taught some children in her cottage home near a trout stream. Chapter 2 of the book begins: "A mile off, and a thousand feet down. So Tom found it: though it seemed as if he could have chucked a pebble on to the back of the woman in the red petticoat who was weeding in the garden..."

Was Lewthwaite Crag the immense Malham Cove? Or could it have been the great scar above Arncliffe—a scar where the white-tailed sea eagle nested? The village name is said to be derived from erne-cliff. Perhaps Lewthwaite was a bit of both.

Tom would have been killed if he had attempted to descend the Cove itself. Of those who have deliberately taken a tumble, none has survived. Instead, Tom found himself on the terraces of the Yoredale Series of rocks. He bumped down a two-foot step of limestone. "Then another bit of grass and flowers. Then bump down a one-foot step. Then another bit of grass and flowers for fifty yards, as steep as the house-roof, where he had to slide down carefully..."

Reaching a "neat pretty cottage" he glanced through the open door which was all hung round with clematis and roses. He saw, within the cottage, an empty fire-place which was filled with a pot of sweet herbs. And there sat "the nicest old woman that ever was seen, in her red petticoat and short dimity bedgown, and clean white cap, with a black silk handkerchief over it, tied under her chin. There was a cat at her feet and twelve or fourteen chubby little children learning their Chris-cross-row..."

Kingsley had tea at Bridge House with Miss Hammond, a little old lady, one of a family who had lived in the village since the end of the sixteenth century and who built Amerdale House, the name Amerdale preceding Littondale as the name of the valley. Wordsworth wrote of "the deep fork of

Amerdale''. The Skirfare, river of the dale, joins the Wharfe at Amerdale Dub. A few tales are still told about Miss Hammond, who was taken to church in a wheelchair. At Bridge House, cleanliness came immediately after godliness. The flagged floors were scoured using sand taken from the side of the river.

Charles Kingsley, on his visit to Bridge End, would surely stroll across the garden to the river's edge, looking for fish. The lady of Bridge End today is Mary Miller, widow of Marmaduke Miller, who was mine-host of The Falcon Hotel in the village. M'duke was a considerable artist and his letterhead, which he designed and drew himself, emphasised the quality of the trout-fishing.

It included a testimony to the Falcon by Halliwell Sutcliffe, author of *The Striding Dales:* ''I know few houses in the five Dales of Yorkshire that are easier to stay at, harder to leave...''

Pam the Fiddler

Threshfield School, in a byroad just across the Wharfe from Grassington, is a solitary building, about sixty feet long, with three bays. Here is a standard Dales building of the seventeenth century building, with stout greystone walls, a roof of stone flags, mullioned windows (which once had shutters) and a single storey porch.

INSIDE the school, three or four light windows illuminate a single lofty room. A blocked off fireplace protrudes incongruously from the west wall at well above human height. Originally, there were two upper rooms for the schoolmaster, the whole enclosed with open ground used as a garden. Last century, when the master ceased to use the upper rooms, the floor was removed, admitting more light to the school. The garden became a playground.

Threshfield School has a resident ghost, Old Pam, transformed by Halliwell Sutcliffe to Pam the Fiddler, who met his death at the hands of a Rector of Linton. Upset by the constant fiddling; the Rector threw a few blows and Pam died, only to return to play his fiddle unto eternity.

Pam is regarded by the children with respectul awe. A folklorist thinks of him with delight. Historians regard his ghost with derision. Old Pam of Victorian times was a ghost full of mischief and merriment. According to the Rev Bailey Harker, writing over a century ago, he would light up the

Threshfield School

school at nights and carry on strange orgies. ''As if in convivial company of the same character as himself, he would fiddle and dance through the midnight hours like one of the sprites of Bacchus.''

Should one of the reverend schoolmasters leave the manuscript of his sermon the desk, added Harker, ''it would be found next morning to have been subjected to the most wanton liberties. One of the terrors held out to children who might be inclined to go by the school on winter evenings was 'Old Pam will get you'.''

In a modern story, it was said that people who passed Threshfield School at dead of night saw lighted candles. Looking through the windows, they saw Pam's ghost fiddling, the audience consisting of dancing imps. One man sneezed. Old Pam and his friends chased him. He escaped by jumping into the Lady Well, which was holy. When I last called at the school, the children believed that Pam lives on in the false roof, but he may have been driven away when a new roof was provided in 1970.

Is there a mysterious Someone at Threshfield School? A former headmistress related that when she was working late, with a light burning, next morning someone was sure to mention the "mysterious" light. Years ago, when she decided to start a parents' association, she was told not to bother because "nobody goes down there at night."

Spectral Dog in Trollers Gill

Take the B6160 Upper Wharfedale road to Barden Tower, cross the Wharfe by the old narrow bridge and motor on to the junction near Appletreewick, where you bear right for Parcevall Hall. Tour the gardens (a charge is made) and then walk down to the entrance and turn right to visit Trollers Gill, the haunt of the barguest, a spectral hound.

IN NORTHERN folklore, spectral hounds are two-a-penny. They have been reported from Ireland to Finland and for all I know may be at plague proportions in the Soviet Union. The Dales hounds are characterised by having eyes as big as saucers and/or balls of fire. Some hounds have reconciled themselves to walking into eternity dragging chains. Whatever happens, don't tease the barguest. John Lambert of Skyrethornes tormented it and was picked up dead.

The Rev Bailey J Harker, in a guide to the Grassington area (1890), wrote that a Wharfedale hound which dragged a chain had eyes which "glistened with unearthly fire". The parson had not himself seen the barguest. It was not that he was scared. He just had a vivid imagination and stayed at home at the very mention of the beast.

Wharfedale had a family of spectral dogs. Or had more than the average number of topers. There was nothing like the proverbial skin-ful to set the spectral dogs off on the prowl. They became the Dales equivalent of the pink elephant. Billy Blakey met a hound unexpectedly when he arrived home at Linton. The beast was sitting on his doorstep. Billy, unlike the parson, was not intimidated and simply said: "Git up an' stir thysel". Or words to that effect.

Charley Simpson, passing Grass Wood one Sunday night, having taken a preaching appointment in the upper dale, had reached the middle of the wood when he heard footsteps—*pit-pat, pit-pat*—which led him to believe he was being followed by the barguest. Quickening his pace, he became aware that Something was keeping up with him. Charley began to run. He could not throw off his pursuer. When he arrived at Bull Ing, where a stream crosses the road, the sounds stopped. Charley did not slacken his pace—and he fell over his tormentor, which was Jackey Hargreaves' donkey!

Some fearsome dogs were mistaken for the barguest. This happened when a Wharfedale farmer shot a very large beast and heared it depart amid the rattle of a chain. On the following day, people were wondering who had slain the great dog from Netherside Hall, which had broken free from its kennel.

Trollers Gill is the classic area for glimpsing the barguest, a name which means mountain demon. As lately as 1881, an Appletreewick man went out to confront the barguest and next morning his body, horribly marked, was found by shepherds.

Halliwell Sutcliffe, in his ultra-romantic style, of a visitor to Trollers Gill who saw the barguest emerge into moonlight. "He'd a shaggy sort o'smell as he went by, and I counted myself for dead. But he changed not to glimpse me, praise all the saints that ever were." This dalesman must have had some Irish blood in him.

The area of Parcevall Hall is haunted by John (Swift Nick) Nevison, the ubiquitous highwayman, and presumably trolls were to be found in the gill which bears their name, though just where they have their subterranean home is not known. It might have been in Hell Hole, a "swallow" above Skyreholme Dam. The pothole opens into a large oblong chamber. Members of the Yorkshire Ramblers' Club descended into it in June, 1896. No trolls were recovered.

Many moons have waxed and waned since anyone saw a spectral hound. Ella Pontefract wrote that "to see the shaggy, dog-like creature in Trollers Ghyll means death, unless there is water between you and it." Guy Ragland Phillips claimed that that red eyes or ears (and the barguest has red eyes) are a characteristic of beings from the Other World in ancient Celtic mythology.

Go to Trollers Gill on a summer day, when the barguest is in its warm-weather haunts on the high fells, and you will be enchanted by this little rocky gorge, the sides of which hold a mass of dancing harebells.

Wee Folk at Elbolton

The map shows Elbolton as a prominent circular hill to the west of Thorpe, the "hidden hamlet" with narrow approach roads and best visited from the B6160, between Threshfield and Burnsall. A footpath to Elbolton begins where the road system ends. The walk is relatively short and not difficult.

ELBOLTON, near the hamlet of Thorpe, is one of the famous reef-knolls, known to Neolithic man who hunted with weapons tipped with flint and might then light a fire for some rudimentary cooking. Elbolton provides a perfect setting for fairies, being quiet and secluded.

Victorian readers of Bailey J Harker's *Guide to Grassington* found the fairies were listed under folklore. Wrote the cleric:

"Fairies, ghosts, omens, charms and many other things that make up beliefs in country districts, were common in the folk-lore of Grassington. Much else that is curious and weird yet remains." Such as the Rev Harker.

The Grassington Fairies were lively creatures, capable of much good or much harm. "Like Robin Hood's foresters they were generally dressed in woodland or Lincoln green; and like the conies (rabbits) dwelt in the rocks. They were spoken of as making their home at Cove Scar—where there is a place still called the Fairy Hole—and at Elbolton. Late at night, and

at early morn, they would come out from their retreats and dance in rings which would be marked by a richer growth of grass than in the rest of the meadows, and in these would spring, as if by magic, hosts of mushrooms."

Mr Harker had these fairies playing pranks on the cattle of the farmer who had grieved them, or they would "blast with mildew his standing corn. They would steal into dairies and turn the milk all sour, or affect the cream so that it would produce no butter, however long it might be churned."

Fairy pipes, curiously-shaped pipes with small bowls and short mouth-pieces, had been picked up. The notion of a fairy with nicotine-stained wings is one of the most delightful pieces of Dales folklore. Let us leave Elbolton with the image of dancing fairies. They sometimes invited a spectator to join their dance. The invitation must not be refused.

A man who danced with the fairies, and who even picked up one of the wee folk and put it in his pocket, had quite a job persuading his wife it had happened. He had the florid look of the ale-swiller. And his pocket was empty.

By the Strid

Use the special Strid Car park provided by Bolton Abbey estate. It is signposted beside the B6160 to the south of Barden Tower. A good footpath leads down to the riverside at the Strid. Do not venture too near the river, for wet rocks are slippery. And on no account attempt to leap across.

> THAT fearful chasm,
> How tempting to bestride!
> For lordly Wharfe is there pent in
> With rocks on either side.

So wrote Wordsworth, after visiting Bolton Abbey in the summer of 1807. The visitor from Grasmere, who doubtless had the company of his sister, Dorothy, ventured into Strid Wood and stood beside the channel through which the Wharfe appears to boil and bubble. Wordsworth's lines, which capture the savage character of this tortured reach of the river, appear in his poem *The Force of Prayer; or The Founding of Bolton Priory,* where he related the curious legend of how a fatal accident at the Strid resulted in the establishment of Bolton Priory near 800 years ago.

But first, let us consider the Strid, a name which may be derived from stryth, referring not so much to the possiblity of a foolhardy person striding from one bank of the river to the other as from the tumultuous rush of the waters. At the

Strid, the River Wharfe, in the early manhood of its life, is constricted by a gritstone channel which stretches for almost a quarter of a mile. Although it is only a few feet wide, the channel is deep, thirty or more feet, with the rocks worn into cave-like hollows.

The Strid is a mossy spot. It has also gathered about it the moss of imaginative story-telling. Legends abound. On the morning of May Day before any fatal accident occurs, a spectral white horse, steed of the queen of the fairies, is to be seen arising from the spray and mist.

A long pointed rock sloping down from the bank at the narrowest part is the Strid Jump. It was an accident here, half-way through the twelfth century, which is said to have resulted in the establishment of Bolton Priory. Fourteen years after William Fiz-Duncan had defeated the troops of King Stephen in the battle of Clitheroe, David, King of Scotland, established him in the Honour of "Skipton and Crafna". Lady Romille bore him two sons and three daughters.

The elder son was survived by the Boy of Egremond, a youth who was fond of hunting. One day, with a greyhound at leash, he strode through Strid Wood and, anxious to reach the other bank of the river, he leapt across the foaming water, as he might have done before, but this day his dog held back. The Boy fell into the river and was drowned.

When an attendant returned to the mother, Lady Aaliza, with news of the tragedy, she was heartbroken. The Augustinian canons of Embsay persuaded her to create a fitting memorial to her lost son by sponsoring their move from (draughty) Embsay to (sheltered) Bolton, in the valley of the Wharfe. It is an attractive tale but among the signatories of those who made the monastic move possible was that of—the Boy of Egremond.

Monks at Bolton Abbey

Leave the A59 at a roundabout and follow the B6160 for a short distance towards Bolton Abbey. A prominent signpost (left) indicates a parking area. Use this park for there is limited space elsewhere. Then cross the road in the village to the Hole in the Wall, the usual approach to Bolton Priory (it was never an Abbey).

BOLTON by the Wharfe is a heavenly place. Morning sunlight gives a yellow tinge to Bolton Hall, a residence of the Duke of Devonshire which has, at its core, the old Priory gatehouse. Light picks out the fine detail of the Priory Church, the former nave, spared at the Dissolution of the Monasteries because it was being used for public worship. Beams of light quest among the remains of the ruined part of the Priory.

Bolton Abbey, situated where Wharfedale broadens and becomes park-like, is one of the Dales honeypots, visited by myriad people each summer. There is always someone following the well-established paths by the river or through the woods. The ghosts of Bolton include the four-legged variety—a roe deer (the celebrated White Doe of Rylstoes, which accompanied Emily Norton to services at the Priory) and the afforementioned white horse (which rises from the surging waters of the Strid on May Day).

Go to Bolton on a misty day in November and you might just see a ghost. If not, there's always a cordial welcome at the Priory Church, where in addition to the Rector there is an enthusiastic team of volunteer guides.

Old-time writers found ghosts romantic. Halliwell Sutcliffe, in *The Striding Dales* (1929) wrote of presences at Bolton Priory: "If you would take courage in both hands...choose the hour between sundown and the murk of dusk, and roam with a quiet heart among the Priory ruins. You may hear the water-wheel going *rub-a-dub-dub* again as it grinds the garnered corn. Big-throated chants of praise may take you unawares, and far-off cries of shepherds to their dogs..."

In the spring of 1973, some amateur archaeologists called off their search in Bolton Priory for the burial place of John de Clifford (The Butcher) who was slain in the Wars of the Roses, 1461. During the search a lady member of the team had been confronted by a man clad in medieval costume, and another spoke of a vision of something "very black and very evil" at the mouth of a tomb they had been excavating.

In a grave they excavated in the south transept of the ruins they found the skeleton of a woman. The tomb was re-sealed and the strange experiences ceased. A team member, entering the church alone, had to leave because he felt something "strong and very frightening".

The most famous and best-documented of the Yorkshire ghosts is that of an Augustinian canon who has appeared fairly often at Bolton Priory. A note about this being appeared in *Lord Halifax's Ghost Book,* published in 1936. Some distinguished people who stayed at the Hall in 1912 guaranteed the authenticity of the story. They were King George V, the Duke of Devonshire, his son (the Marquis of Hartington) and Lord Desborough.

The Marquis, then a boy on vocation from Eton, and up at Bolton (as were the others) for the grouse-shooting, had been accommodated at the Rectory, which is believed to stand on the site of the Priory guest house. He went to his bedroom at 11-15 pm on August 18 and saw a figure standing at the door.

The apparition was "dressed in nondescript clothes and was more or less clean-shaven. I was at the top of the staircase, looking down the passage in which mine was the end room. I went downstairs again and fetched another light, but on going up again the figure had disappeared." The ghost had been discussed that evening but the Marquis was not present at the talk and he was not thinking about a ghost when he went upstairs.

Further information was given to Lord Halifax by the Duchess of Devonshire, who had quizzed her son. "He seems to be the same man who was seen two or three times by the Vicar, but the Vicar's ghost wore a brown dress and Eddy declares this man was dark grey or black. Eddy's ghost had a round face—no beard, but what was described as a rough face. When we asked the Vicar afterwards if his ghost had a beard he said 'No' but that he looked as if he had not shaved for four or five days, and his face was very round." (A Rector, not a Vicar, has the spiritual oversight at Bolton).

On this last point, the Marquis was wrong. White (or un-dyed wool) was the rainment of the Cistercians, the Augustinians being known as "black canons". A more recent sighting of the ghost disclosed that clothing was a black cassock-like robe with a woollen white overlay, black cloak and flat black hat. Augustinian canons were not subject to tonsure (the stylised clipping of the hair on the head) and were allowed to grow beards if they wished.

At the time when *Lord Halifax's Ghost Book* was published, the Rev C F Tomlinson was a relatively new Rector. During his long stay at Bolton Abbey he did not hear or see anything inexplicable at the Rectory. A former agent of the estate, Mr A Downs, told in 1936 that Lord Charles Cavendish mentioned seeing the ghost about 1920. And Mrs Etchells, of Bolton Bridge Cottages, related that about 1896, when she was a child, her playmates spoke of the Rectory ghost by the name of Punch.

The Rev James MacNabb, one-time Rector of Bolton Abbey, was standing by the window in an empty bedroom of the Rectory in 1911 when he turned round and saw an apparition standing in the doorway. As the Rector moved, the monkish figure vanished. Was it, as some claimed, the figure was of a monk who was murdered for the sake of relics he had been carrying from one community to another. The body was thrown into a space in the walls of the Rectory.

So to the present day. A young doctor who for a time commuted between a cottage in the upper dale and Leeds, was motoring near Bolton Hall at daybreak when he was intrigued to see several figures in black habits walking beside the road. A visitor to the Priory Church reported seeing a figure in the old choir. And a Rector who seems to have been ultra-sensitive to ghostly matters told me he was sawing wood in the cellar at the Rectory when he distinctly heard the *slap, slap* of sandalled feet moving across the floor above him. As far as he knew, he was alone in the house.

The White Doe

Skipton Castle, home of the illustrious Cliffords, is open daily except on Christmas Day. Norton Tower, used by the ill-fated Nortons, is a ruined structure perched on spur of Crookrise and visible (left) to those who motor between Rylstone and Skipton on the B6265. The location of Bolton Abbey is mentioned in the previous note.

EVERYONE loves a mystery. The White Doe is a sixteenth century whodonit. What are the circumstances behind William Wordsworth's tale of a white doe which appeared at

Bolton Priory during divine service? When Wordsworth visited Wharfedale and planned to write a long poem based on Bolton Abbey, his main requirement was for a romantic theme. The Rev William Carr, Rector of Bolton Abbey, referred him to a tale told by Thomas Dunham Whitaker in his *History of Craven*.

The story concerns the ill-fated Norton family, who held at Rylstone until, early in the seventeeth century, the area was granted to their arch enemies, the Cliffords of Skipton. In the story, Emily Norton had a white doe, given to her by her brother Francis. When Francis died, young Emily regularly walked from Rylstone to Bolton Priory on Sundays.

BOLTON Abbey

The white doe lingered by the grave of Francis Norton during Divine Service and then followed Emily back home. No date was given. Legends are allowed to float free from a literary straightjacket. The type of deer—roe or fallow—is not specified. A good story can be spoiled by an injection of raw science.

The White Doe of Rylstone is associated with the Pilgrimage of Grace, a rebellion by northern Catholics against the Dissolution of the Monasteries. The action would be about 1540. Wordsworth, charmed by the tale, and having vivid images of Bolton's dukal grandeur, returned to Grasmere and composed his long poem, *The White Doe of Rylstone*, which is by no means his finest work.

Emily Norton was ubiquitous. She bobs up in another Dales tradition—that of Lile Emily's Bridge, over a tributary beck of the Wharfe. Emily is supposed to have used it when attending church at Linton, not Bolton. And (let it be whispered) Emily does not appear in the long pedigree of the Norton family. Hers was not a Norton family name.

Francis, her "brother", most certainly lived, though he took no part in the Pilgrimage of Grace, being a Protestant. He is thought to have been murdered by resentful folk on Barden Fell and was buried at Bolton Priory. So we are left with a white doe, which was presumably an albino. If you visit Towneley Hall, at Burnley, you will see a most charming statue of Emily and her unusual pet.

Was Norton Tower, on Crookrise, a fortified structure connected with the often fierce squabbling between the Nortons and their neighbours the Cliffords? Or could it have been as Arthur Raistrick, the Dales antiquary thought, "a rather jolly summer house?"

Three Peaks

Trolls and Things

Leave the A65 by turning right, just beyond Cowan Bridge, and you are on a stretch of road marked grandly on the map as "Roman Road". It enfolds in long straight stretches, but this route has hardly outgrown the status of a country lane. It is flanked by tall hedges and eventually forks, one branch crossing a bridge over a long-lost railway and dropping into Lunesdale. The other branch extends Barbondale, where our witch hunt will begin. (A cul de sac from the aforementioned minor road goes directly to Bull Pot Farm, two minutes walk from the pothole with witchly associations, but why spoil a glorious expedition by making it too easy?).

THE CREATURES popularly associated with our northern caves are trolls, fairies and boggarts. Superstitious folk gave the underworld a wide berth. Some thought that the potholes were vents through which water poured at the time of the Flood, when Noah sailed the waves. In the area you are about to visit are systems with truly romantic names—Fairy Holes, Boggart's Roaring Holes and Bull Pot of the Witches.

Motor up Barbondale until you see a fingerpost (right) pointing out a bridleway to Bull Pot. In summer, the rocky path is a well-trodden route between two rustling expanses of bracken which, by October, has taken on a copper hue. The open track becomes a green road when, having passed through a gate, the route is flanked by drystone walls. Thorn trees grow from funnel-shaped holes known as "swallows".

None of them has supernatural associations.

Bull Pot farmhouse, now owned by English Nature and leased to the Red Rose Cave and Pothole Club, caters for those who, like Orpheus, are happiest when in the Underworld, in this case several long cave systems and their catchment areas, including Easegill Caverns, the longest cave system in Britain (and the 11th longest in the world). The water which continues the process of widening the caverns goes to ground by way of fourteen major sink holes.

A fingerpost at Bull Pot farm indicates Easegill. A few minutes away, on the right, is what appears to be a small deciduous wood, surrounded by a drystone wall. The trees have sprouted around Bull Pot of the Witches. You may wonder if witches roost in trees during the day and your glance may be towards the wall, in case one of the witches left her jet-propelled beson propped against it.

There were no witches there in 1820, when a correspondent of the *Lonsdale Magazine* arrived in the district, for he assured ''the timid reader'' that all the witches ''which formerly haunted this dirty, gloomy cavern are either dead or banished to the Highlands of Scotland, where they frequently cross the path of a Scott or a Hogg.'' Our correspondent asked a local man about the name of the caves and was told: ''I never sa' any witches, but me grandmuddar said at a parshall a witches ust to meet yance a year e thor hoals, an mead a girt feast, an neabody mud gang tull it, but sic as thersels.''

The old writer was correct when he stated that Easegill's Witches Caves are dirty and gloomy. In the entrance to one of them he wrote: ''To the right we found a pool of water, to the left a pool of mud, and in the middle a mixture of both. The cave is nothing but cracks and crannies among the loose strata of the limestone.'' He lamented that the witches had left the place full of water. Looking into the hole from the track, I could not imagine the popular type of witch, a woman with crooked nose, black hat and clothes—not forgetting the cat—inhabiting such a place.

Bull Pot of the Witches, 210 ft deep, was visited by the Balderstons of Ingleton in 1888. He was a "retired professor of sciences" with a flair for local associations who in a book put in the location of potholes in relation to the pattern of walls, a handy form of reference. The Balderstons described Bull Pot of the Witches as "a dreadful hole, foetid with the dead carcasses of sheep and lambs, and whitened with skeletons. A vast cave-like mouth is to be seen in the base of its north-western side."

The Balderstons went to Rumbling Hole, on Leck Fell, and afterwards wrote: "But hark! *tap, tap, tap,* comes slowly from the distant depths; this is the home of the gnomes or fairies; they are at work below in their workshop, and a far-off hammering can be heard. Leave them in peace! Some day the good fays may work your weal, although the ill-natured have designated as Rumbling Hole what we prefer to dream of as The Fairies Workshop."

The footpath continues to Easegill, a watercourse with rounded stones on its bed. Normally water thunders into Easegill Kirk, where the limestone has been eroded into smooth shapes creating an impression of a church. In time of drought, a visitor might walk on the dry bed of the beck and clamber without too much difficulty into the kirk, where the "walls" overhang and a U-shaped rift allows the explorer to see a smooth rock face, like an altar.

The only "worshippers" in this natural kirk are wild birds. A wren's voice resounds as in an echo chamber. The chacking of ring ouzels in late summer is from birds stripping thorns of their berries before the birds follow a migration route to the Atlas Mountains of North Africa. It is a journey which would make one of the local witches envious.

A Dentdale Mansion

> Whernside Manor, formerly known as West House, stands
> off the back road between Dent Town and Cowgill. A spen-
> did Georgian facade is visible to motorists travelling updale
> but may not be noticed by travellers in the other direction.

WEST HOUSE was built for yeoman family called Sill, some
of whom migrated to the West Indies. One branch of the Sills
owned plantations in Jamaica and it has long been claimed in
Dentdale that West House was constructed using the last of
the slave labour to be employed in England.

Through the years, West House fell into disrepair. Then, in
1940, it was restored by Sir Albert Braithwaite, a landowner
with quarry interests. It was Sir Albert who gave the mansion
its present name. In more recent times it became a caving centre, organising courses and having adequate accommodation
for students.

Stories are told of old-time slaves, who are said to have
bathed in Black Dub, a sinister pool below Rigg End. A negro
who fell in love with one of the daughters of the Sill family
is said to have drowned there. When the bill to abolish
slavery was passed, the owners of West House, unable to
maintain their captives, were thrown into underground
passages beneath the manor and left without food and water.

A nameless young woman who was trapped with the
slaves has evolved into the Grey Lady. Perhaps it was she
who kept a young woman student awake in one of the dor-
mitories of the caving centre. She did not see anyone but
awoke to hear a creaking sound, as though someone was
walking round and round the room. While the others slept,
she remained sitting in bed, wondering if the strange sounds
would return.

One of the hoary tales of Whernside Manor is of the time
when alterations were being carried out and two carpenters

had the place to themselves at a time when there was a defect in the electricity system. They worked into gathering darkness, completing an urgent job, and by the time they had finished, the darkness was absolute. One man fumblingly gathered together the tools. The other made his way down the rear stairs of the Manor. He heard his workmate's cries high above: "Hang on. Its pitch black. Wait for me."

The first man, continuing his descent, felt a hand in his. He was still holding the hand when he reached the yard outside the Manor. A voice behind him cried out once again: "Hang on. Wait for me."

His workmate had not yet reached the foot of the stairs.

Mystery of Masongill House

Masongill, reached along a narrow, hedge-bordered road which extends eastwards from the A65 between Ingleton and Cowan Bridge, is during the summer curtained by deciduous leaves. The road continues up the fellside, near Marble Steps pothole, its position indicated by a collection of geriatric trees, some of which have been toppled by gales. Sir Arthur Conan Doyle, who was very familiar with these austere uplands, believed they might have a population of fairies.

IN THE STORY of Masongill House, unanswered questions abound. This was for many years the home of the Wallers. Following the death of Bryan Charles Waller, in 1932, the servants were instructed by Ada Waller, his widow, to empty the attic of personal papers, including notebooks and diaries. These must be taken to the back of the house, where a bonfire had been made.

A young lady who worked at the House glanced at one of the notebooks. In it, Ada Waller had written of her often intolerable life as the wife of the man who was virtually the Squire of Masongill. The servant felt guilty and very sad at prying into the affairs of the family. She hurled the book on to the bonfire. So perished in flames the precise details of a fascinating story involving Bryan Charles Waller, and his wife, who as the former Miss Anderson, from St Andrews, who had come to the district as governess at Thornton-in-Lonsdale Vicarage.

Thornton-in-Lonsdale

This story also involves Mary Doyle, a widow whom Waller first met in Edinburgh and saw much of during her twenty years of residence in Masongill. Mary was the mother of Sir Arthur Conan Doyle who, as the world knows, was the author of early whodunnits and creator of Sherlock Holmes, the sleuth whose first inquiries were detailed in *The Strand Magazine* in 1891.

One would need a man with the acute perception of Holmes to unravel the Mysteries of Masongill House. It is not the type of Victorian melodrama which involves cobwebs, shrieks in the night and bloodstained hands. Was Conan Doyle really the doctor's son? It is improbable. Was his younger sister, who was nicknamed Dodo, fathered by Dr Waller? Maybe. Or not. Mary Doyle, who occupied the nearest cottage to the big house, was known to have been on cordial relations with Waller. Was his love for her more than platonic? Were the early morning visits, across the grass, from Masongill House to her cottage, merely to inquire about her health?

Each family—the Doyles and Wallers—had an illustrious background, with strong literary connections. The Wallers, who had roots in Kent and Buckinghamshire, took up regular residence at Masongill about the year 1840 when the estate was bequeathed to a Mr Nicholas Procter by his great uncle, Bryan Waller, on condition he assumed the names and arms of Waller. He complied and moved here, marrying one of the Procter family.

In his time, the House had a magnificent library of several thousand volumes, including Robert Southey's *The Doctor* which, published anonymously and with a scene set in the Ingleton district, was for a time thought to have been penned by Waller. He knew Southey and was also a friend of Wordsworth and the two Coleridges. Nicholas died in 1877 and was interred at Thornton-in-Lonsdale. His wife, Julia Perry Waller, followed him to the grave two months later.

Bryan Charles Waller, who was born at Masongill House on July 27, 1853, was until the early 1890s an MD who lectured at Edinburgh University. (He was known to Masongill folk as The Professor). He first met Mrs Doyle in Edinburgh. Mrs Doyle had married the artist Charles Altamont Doyle, who was a brilliant man despite being an alcoholic and an epileptic. When he became mentally ill, in about 1883, he was committed to a mental home near Dumfries, where he spent the next ten years, eventually swallowing his tongue during a fit.

Mary and the children had moved to Masongill in about 1883. The state of health of Mr Doyle was kept secret from local people, who presumed Mary Doyle to be a widow. In her prime, she was a pert and physically attractive woman. Her literary interests would make her a delightful companion to a bookish person like Waller, for her brother-in-law, Richard Doyle, had designed the cover of *Punch* and she knew Thackeray, also Williams, a member of the publishing house which handled works by Charlotte Bronte.

Three of Mrs Doyle's children were married at Thornton-in-Lonsdale church, which is surprising in view of the Doyle's background in Catholicism. Conan Doyle, the first to be married, became a spiritualist and took a serious view of fairies, being enchanted by the stories which reached him of the wee creatures being photographed at Cottingley, and theorising that the hills behind Masongill were likely to have a fairy population.

On August 6, 1885, the church register reveals that Arthur Conan Doyle married Louisa Hawkins. In December of that year Jane Adelaide Rose Doyle married Nelson Foley, a widower. Then, on April 11, 1899, Bryan Mary Josephine Julia Doyle took as her husband one Charles Cyril Ansell.

Conan Doyle visited Masongill from time to time. Over the years, he wrote an estimated 1,500 letters to his mother. He loved to wander on the moors behind Masongill, and in one letter he noted: ''We strolled over the moors in the mornings or stood upon the Moorstone Crag (probably Hunts Cross) to watch the red sun sinking beneath the distant waters of Morecambe.'' I can imagine him peering into Marble Steps, the deep gash in limestone and the haunt of goodness knows how many strange creatures.

Doyle had introduced his famous character Sherlock Holmes to the public in *A Study in Scarlet,* published in 1887. What connection was there, apart from the name, between the fictional Sherlock and the names of two local clergymen—the Rev T Sherlock of Ingleton and the Parson Sherlock who had spiritual supervision at Bentham? Did Conan Doyle quietly lift these surnames and convert them into Christian names for his super-sleuth?

Tongues doubtless wagged as Dr Waller tripped across the

greensward from Masongill House to the cottage housing Mary Doyle, though he was said to have placed a bell in the cottage and he rang it when he wished to see her. Those were the active years. Towards the end of his life, Dr Waller was scarcely capable of walking. He spent much of his time in bed and during the winter he rarely left the house.

Village children were not allowed to play within view of the building, a large cupboard blocked those kitchen windows from which the lawn could be overlooked by the servants and Waller's bedroom was considered sacred. Report had it that his bedside table was forever littered with pills and potions. If he wanted any of them he made no effort to get it, but rapped his stick on the floor, then using the stick to point out the object he desire.

As with most people who had lived frugally, Waller became stingy with others in old age. His shirts were made of flannel by the children of Westhouse School, who used herringbone stiches for collars and cuffs. The doctor's last appearance in Ingleton was one voting day. He drove into Ingleton in a dog cart. The frail old man was swaddled in blankets, his feet resting on a metal hot water bottle covered with carpeting. The bottle had been filled moments before his departure from home.

Mary Doyle left Masongill in about 1920 and died, at the grand age of 83, at the home of her famous son, who was now Sir Arthur Conan Doyle. He died in 1930. Waller breathed his last on November 14, 1932. He had left instructions that his body should be conveyed to Thornton church in his much-loved dog cart, but this was found to be unsafe. The church bier was trundled from House to Church. Tenants helped to fill in the grave. One of them looked into the hole onto the coffin of the martinet and remarked: "Now then, there'll be no 'yes, sir' and 'no, sir' where you've gone."

Mrs Waller lived on for a few more years. She was inclined to snobbery. At least she could be herself rather than, as before, having to be at the beck-and-call of the husband who tormented her. The windows of Masongill House were shuttered and barred. The sight of a servant walking through a dark house with a paraffin lamp, closing creaky shutters, would have appealed to the imagination of Conan Doyle.

The former servant girl who told me about the burning of the family records also related that when Mrs Waller was alive, the deadline for servants to be back in the House was 10 p.m. One February night in 1933, she and her young man walked hurriedly from Ingleton to Masongill in a blizzard. The approaching deadline gave wings to their feet. The man recalled that on his return to Ingleton he saw Thornton church burning like a torch.

Mrs Waller redrafted her will several times as the beneficiaries predeceased her. When she died, the remains were cremated. The ashes should have been scattered on the fells behind Masongill—across the high open ground on which she was fond of walking when the tension at home was near to breaking point. Ironically, the ashes were placed in Dr Waller's grave. At first, the gravedigger mistakenly began to open the wrong grave.

A woman visiting her family grave pointed out the error, an appropriate climax to a mysterious story.

North Ribblesdale

Some Railway Ghosts

The Settle-Carlisle Railway has a length of rather more than seventy-two miles, one-third of the line being in Yorkshire. The B6479 extends north of Settle and keeps close company with the Settle-Carlisle, through Horton and Selside, all the way to Ribblehead, where it joins the old Lancaster-Richmond turnpike road (B6255). There is ample parking at Ribblehead. A well-used footpath is within easy distance of tracks all the way to Blea Moor signal box and continues (for those with the will and energy) right over Blea Moor to Dent Head.

BLEA MOOR had its ghost, a hob, long before the Settle-Carlisle Railway was built in the 1870s. The lile ghost used to wait for a cart to pass along the open road between Gearstones and Newby Head. He would then jump on the cart and have a ride. Whether or not he took to riding locomotives I do not know.

During the construction period of the railway (1869-1876) hundreds of workers were housed at so-called shanties on the moor to the east of Ribblehead viaduct. A hospital was provided and had to be extended during a smallpox outbreak. In due course, as the shanties were being dismantled, visitors to the hospital made a thorough examination, also entering the dead-house (mortuary).

One of the party lifted the lid from a new coffin and was startled to find it contained a body. Had the authorities forgotten to bury him? The Coroner must be informed.

Another visitor approached the coffin and, in order to deduce if the flesh was rigid or flabby, pinched the man's left leg. The "corpse" raised his head and cried out: "Can't you let a poor fellow sleep quietly?"

Dent Head

Blea Moor
Tunnel

Ribblehead

It was a navvy who had been sleeping off the effects of a night's hard drinking. He was told that, while in a stupor, he might have been buried alive. In any case, that coffin was us-ed for the reception of people who had been suffering from smallpox and fevers. The navvy asked for thruppence, so that he could get another pint of beer. He then inquired the way to Keighley. (Incidentally, the hospital buildings were not sold with other Midland properties but were put to the torch).

Dick Fawcett told me that newcomers to a permanent way gang were soon introduced to the local ghosts and were sent on silly missions. A ganger at Ribblehead had a shock when he saw a new member of the gang running towards Blea Moor with carpet slippers on his feet. Breathlessly he said he must "stop t'express". One of the gang, who was teasing him, even went to his hut and loaned the lad some slippers so that he could run faster.

George Horner, for many years a signalman at Blea Moor box, which stands in grand isolation beside a windswept stretch of the line between Ribblehead Viaduct and Blea Moor tunnel, was glad he was not of a nervous disposition. In winds, the old box cracked and creaked. "If I heard the steps creaking, I'd no idea who it might be. I entertained Bishop Treacy to cups of tea."

When on duty, George, who was living at Selside at the time, parked his van by one of the piers at the north end of the viaduct and walked up the lineside to the box. It was invariably windy. A westerly gale, sweeping up from the Irish Sea via the Lune Valley and the narrow, deep valley of Chapel-le-Dale, found its first obstruction in the lanky arches of the viaduct, where it moaned like the sound track of a Bronte film.

George grew accustomed to the solitude, although when the railway was fully used, and all the levers at the box were in action, as he attended to the loop and sidings, there was much coming and going of railwaymen. Platelayers working in the area sometimes left tins of food to be warmed up on the stove. (Once, when one of the gang collected various tins, a platelayer afterwards observed that it was the first time he had eaten pears when they were piping hot).

Once, after dark, a group of walkers who had lost their way arrived at the box, having been attracted by the light. It was yet another windy day. The gusty wind came from the north. Occasionally, when it blew at full strength, it burst open the signal box door. George welcomed the walkers and mischievously told them he was also expecting a ghost.

On such a wild night, the news was greeted with six-inch shivers. One of the party asked what sort of ghost it was. George, sucking his pipe, then talking in an unemotional way, said: "You'll soon find out. It rushes about and now and again bursts open the door." Coincidentally, the wind rose to a shriek. The door was flung open. The box filled with turbulent air. When George had reached the door to close it, he became aware that he was alone in the box. The walkers had fled and were heading across the moor, happier about facing the perils of the night than the shrieking ghost of Blea Moor.

A macabre incident during the £3.5m restoration of Ribblehead Viaduct, which terminated just before Christmas, 1991, was the discovery, propped against one of the parapets, of a coffin from which protruded an arm and hand. The discovery was made by some Irish workmen, who crossed themselves several times, then reported the matter to the Resident Engineer, who made further inquiries. The arm (and it was simply an arm, unattached to a body) was made of rubber. It was just a hoax. When, in due course, the police had investigated and were asked what the contractors might do with the coffin, the reply was: "Burn it!"

Salt Lake Cottages, which began life as accommodation for railway servants and their families, had a ghostly presence, usually to be detected in No.1. This ghost did not wear a white sheet, nor wail at night, being merely a chilly presence. A platelayer who lived there had been killed when struck by a train on the Dent Head length. He left a wife and son. The hauntings began at the time of the accident.

The front bedroom of the house had a special attraction for the ghost which sometimes crept into bed, not unnaturally scaring the occupant. The first time it happened, the awakened sleeper, feeling this ghostly presence (this limited area of intense cold) was unable to move or scream for a while. The tenant of No.2 cottage detected the ghost when he changed from one bedroom to another. He reported: "It was just like being stroked with a big feather duster."

Selside, in North Ribblesdale, is the hamlet through which

motorists drive with care because of the bends in the road. A signal box, manned by women during the 1939-45 war, was dismantled and moved to Steamtown at Carnforth, some years after it had featured in a ghost story with a difference. George Horner, walking from Horton-in-Ribblesdale to Selside to take over his shift at the signal box, was on foot because the ground held fresh snow. He recalls seeing a man moving ahead of him.

The man took the well-used path to the box and his presence did not worry George, who was used to seeing strangers about. His concern began when the figure bypassed the box, crossed the railway lines and vanished from sight. George realised, with a shock of horror, that the only prints in the fresh snow were his. The stranger had vanished literally without trace.

Big John, a Selside ghost usually seen in the period between October to March, was detected in a decrepit building from which strange tappings were heard, as though John was busy cobbling. Kit Sedgwick, who lived in the house next door, and used the decrepit premises, worked on the railway but was a cobbler in his spare time. Kit and his wife were familiar with the tapping which, when it was first heard at the start of a new haunting season, was usually greeted by them with the words: "Hello—t'auld lad's landed back."

One night, Kit, having promised to repair a pair of dancing shoes which were urgently required, went to his workroom and so that villagers would not distract him by calling for a chat, a cobbler's shop being a regular cal-'oil (gossiping place), he locked the outside door, finished the shoes and was standing looking at them when he heard some footsteps on the stairs.

Kit concluded that his wife was coming to tell him his supper was ready. He then recalled that he had locked the door and she could not get in. Kit scampered from the room in fright. As he descended the stairs, he passed through what he later described as "a chilly area". Arriving at his home next door, he heard his wife say: "You look as though you've seen a ghost." Said Kit: "I think I have!"

Kit sat down to eat his supper. The ghostly tapping could be heard. "T'auld lad must have been going to work," said Kit, adding: "And I got in his way."

Witch of Clapdale

Clapham, on the south-western side of the Ingleborough group of fells, lies just off the A65. The village, which is largely owned by the Farrer family of Ingleborough Estate, is neatly divided into two by Clapham beck, which is spanned by several bridges. Clapham has an Information Centre in the holiday season and a capacious car park (for which a charge is made). From here there is a scenically exciting approach on foot to the summit of Ingleborough. One route, a walled lane beside the Woodyard, goes via Clapdale Farm and Ingleborough Cave, thence to Trow Gill, Gaping Gill and up the mountain on a well-worn path. The other is through the Woods (a small charge is made).

IT IS RELATED that Dame Alice Ketyll, who lived in a cottage at the foot of Trow Gill, had a foster son, John de Clapham, who lived at Clapdale Castle. He did not have good fortune, so Alice called on the Devil to help him. Alice had to promise to sweep the old Clapham bridge, near the church, between Compline and Curfew, and repeat the lines:

> *Into the house of John, my sonne,*
> *Hie all the wealth of Clapham towne.*

At midnight she was to take nine red cocks, freshly killed, and place them in a ring round her on the bridge, and to call her familiar spirit (one Robyn Artisson) by name. Robin would appear when called. If the nine red cockerels were not on offer on any night, the Devil would assist her only once more. Then she would be his.

Alice signed the bond with her own blood. The Devil whistled. The familiar spirit appeared, with a grin on his face, knowing that to find nine red cocks each night would be impossible. So Dame Alice became a witch and used her power, while it lasted, to help the Lord of Clapdale Castle. In return, her soul went to the Devil.

Robin Hood's Mill

Back to North Ribblesdale from Clapham, taking a road which leaves the A65 for Austwick and continues within viewing distance of the little private hamlet of Wharfe, under Moughton Hill, and on to Helwith Bridge. When the road shakes off the company of walls and open common is seen (with a large quarry to the left), take a road right and drive to Knight Stainforth, taking a left turn just beyond a large, white-painted hall to reach Stainforth Bridge. Alternatively, continue to Helwith Bridge, cross the bridge which spans river and Settle-Carlisle and keep right for Stainforth, where there is a large car park (complete with honesty box). A road bridge crosses the railway and descends to the bridge.

KNIGHT STAINFORTH HALL and the packhorse-type bridge (which since 1931 has been owned by the National Trust) were built in the 1670s by Samuel Watson, a Quaker, this ending the need for a "stony ford", from which the name Stainforth is derived. The bridge was well used from the moment it was built, being on the packhorse route between York and Lancaster.

Stand on the bridge and look upriver. Notice, on the left bank a heap of stones. This marked the site of Robin Hood's Mill. It was said to have been owned by a man who, in his quest for extra income, kept the grindstones turning on the Sabbath. The bridge sank out of sight, but the grindstones might still be heard rumbling far below ground.

A group of potholers who investigated the phenomenon in the 1930s are blamed for stopping the mill operating by the changes the wrought to the underworld as they explored the cave system. They had been warned by a clergyman that in trying to solve the mystery they might destroy the romance associated with it. The favourite theory of those who did not favour the story of a lost mill was that the rumbling was caused by an underground watercourse. The potholers, including

Tot Lord, excavated the hole to a depth of 10ft to 12ft. The rumbling sound was then to be clearly heard. It ceased as debris fell to lower levels and muffled the sound of the water.

The ghosts of man and dog roam between the Hall and Dog Hill. The ghosts are said to have occupied a hole high on the side of Knight Stainforth Hall, which had several windows blocked off at the time of the unhygienic tax on window space.

Down at Langcliffe, a high wall separates the grounds of the hall from the road, just across which lies Bowerley, a large house now a hotel and conference centre. Several people have testified to the presence of a woman "in an old-fashioned, ankle length dress", crossing the road between the two places. The apparition has used a small gate set in the wall of Langcliffe Hall. A Horton man who was courting a lass from Settle some 45 years ago recalls pedalling his bike like mad as he returned home on that stretch of the road.

A Bone Cave

To reach Victoria Cave, park the car at the head of Langcliffe Brow, where a track leads off to a cattle grid, and walk along the track to a metal gate. Beyond the gate is a sign, pointing right. A step-stile is negotiated then (taking great care, especially in wet weather, when the limestone and clay are very slippery) follow the wallside until a track is seen going diagonally up the screes, just beyond a sign warning visitors not to approach the cave too closely because of the chance of rockfalls. Victoria Cave is revealed as an enormous hole in the cliff face.

I ONCE SAW a ghostly monk enter Victoria Cave. He turned out to be a young man from Bradford who, converting a blanket into a monkish habit, and wearing rope as a belt, had arrived at the cave for a time of fasting and contemplation. Several days later, the "ghost" broke his fast at a local house by demolishing bacon sandwiches and cups of hot tea.

The bone caves of Attermire kept their secrets for an immense amount of time. It was foxes which led to the rediscovery of Victoria Cave, on the scars above Langcliffe. In the year Queen Victoria was crowned, several young men with dogs went to an area of scree where, high up, there were small holes, generally attributed to foxes. A dog was put into one hole and did not immediately reappear. It was heard barking underground, the sound suggesting a space bigger than a fox earth.

Stones were pulled away and one of the lads crawled into a chamber. (He did not know it at the time, but he was the first person to enter it for about a thousand years). He was an apprentice plumber and when he told his master about his find, the plumber himself began to visit the cave in secret and with lights, recovered objects which had lain undisturbed since ancient times.

From the evidence brought to light in what became known as Victoria Cave and other ''dry'' systems in the Settle district, we have a remarkable idea of the ancient fauna and human life in this area. The first cavemen may have been small bands of Azilians, originating in France. They crossed the low-lying plain which is now the North Sea. They have been named after a French cave, the Mas d'Azil, in the Pyrenees, where the best evidence of their activity has been unearthed.

The Azilians knew the limestone country for a long but indefinite period, but they remain mysterious, shadowy figures We cannot even guess at their numbers, but the total human population of England in those days would be a few thousand. About 10,000 years ago, man hunted game, harpooned fish in the lakes left by the Ice Age, or went fowling. We know he lived partly on fish, for one of the Victoria Cave finds was a bone harpoon, with reversed barbs, a little more than three inches long. It was discovered with the broken jaws and bones of the brown bear, red deer, horse and ox.

Early Man would seek protection from the hazards of primeval night in dry caves on the scars. Caves always had an attraction for him, and the main attraction was security in time of trouble. This notion survived until recent times, for in 1745, when the Young Pretender was at Shap and it was doubtful if he would pass through Ribblesdale or by way of Preston, one of the Settle landowners hid his son, and the family plate, in a cave not far from Victoria. He had an idea that the Highlanders were fond of eating children and putting their hands on all precious metals. When there was a threat of Napoleonic invasion, caves were earmarked among local families.

Old Johnny's Ghost

To visit Winskill, leave the car at the park in Stainforth, North Ribblesdale, and follow a path which ascends a relatively steep wooded slope. Or drive up Langcliffe Brow to near a cattle-grid and park at a suitable place. Cross the grid and take an unfenced road almost immediately on the left. It leads to Winskill, where a fingerpost indicates a right of way. Return to the car by the same route, noticing Sampson's Toe (a big erratic, or stone shifted to its present position by glacial action). A footpath from Langcliffe to Stainforth passes the well-preserved kiln of a type invented by a German called Hoffman and continues through a semi-wooded area to reach the road opposite Stainforth youth hostel.

THE HAMLET of Winskill is perched on Winskill Scar, where quarrying has taken place, though since it ceased the face has weathered sufficiently for it to have regained its natural appearance. Tom Twisleton, who lived at Winksill, near Settle, was a Victorian with a fear that the Craven farmer would lose his expressive words. The mother tongue was being spoilt by an improved formal education, by railway transport and the advent of tourism.

The "Winskill Bard", a small-time farmer, developed into a big man, over six feet tall and built in proportion. His association with society came once a week, when he attended the Tuesday market in Settle. He and his brother, who was also a poet, were characters—men with minds of their own—and one Christmas Day they broke the ice and bathed in a local beck.

He told inquirers: "I rhyme 'cos I can't help it." The themes were developed in his mind by day and set down on paper in the evening, when the farm work was done. His topics were various, ranging from an account of the death of a Welshman during the construction of the Settle-Carlisle Railway (1869-76) to a poetic note accompanying an insurance policy to a lady who was scared of fire.

Tom had a collection of poems written in the Craven dialect published in January, 1867, under the title of *Splinters struck off Winskill Rock.* Among the tales was one concerning a man who, befuddled with ale, met a "ghost" on his way home. When he sensed a ghostly presence:

> *His hair began ta bristle,*
> *And stand streight up upon his heead,*
> *Like burrs upon a thistle...*

Subsequently:

> *It mud be t'ghost, he couldn't tell,*
> *That stood i' t'nook to watch him;*
> *Or else it was t'owd lad (the devil) hissel*
> *Hed come up here to catch him;*
> *Saa on his knees he down did fo,*
> *He pray'd loud as a Ranter,*
> *Till t'ghost sprung out fra under t' wo,*
> *An' started off o' t'canter.*

It was, of course a horse, and the moral for topers was:

> *But allus try to get away*
> *Wal t'sun shines breet an' bonny;*

Ye'll ken a horse be t'leet o' day,
An' not be like owd Johnny.

Tom Twisleton died at Burley-in-Wharfedale in 1917. He was living far away from his beloved Winskill and wrote little in his later years.

Beggar's Wife Bridge

> The bridge was once a solitary structure spanning Tems Beck (or the River Tems as some grandly call it) near Four Lane Ends at Giggleswick. The bridge is flanked on both sides by new housing.

THE NAME Beggar's Wife relates to a beggar who went beserk and slew his wife. She came back to her old haunts. A witness described the ghost as "a rushing shape with nothing but a cobweb for her face", adding that she looked fearfully behind her as though the beggar was still in pursuit.

A Big Black Dog

> Wigglesworth is in the Ribble Valley, between Long Preston and Tosside. The stretch of road where the dog appeared to protect the minister is on the B6478, just beyond the Y-junction. At times, the air is heavy with the rotten-egg smell from sulphur wells. The winding road is now shaded by well-grown trees. A narrow bridge encourages caution in motorists before the steady climb on the way to Tosside.

A SERIES of whistles, rising and falling like the piping of a north-country Pan, might be heard by travellers to Tosside, where the road between the Old Vicarage and the School has, since 1974, been the boundary between North Yorkshire and Lancashire. The eerie sounds, which are really high-pitched squeals, with a nasal quality, are heard only in autumn, when the rut or mating season of the sika deer is in progress. At other times, an alarmed deer gives short, sharp squeals.

These are strange sounds in our northern dale-country. Sika deer evolved in Japan and were introduced to the Bowland district to provide sport for the Ribblesdale Buckhounds. The pack was long since disbanded. The deer now running wild in Bowland are the descendants of those which escaped the hunt. A "whistling" stag is really announcing his presence to the hinds, which have been lying up in woodland cover and then, in the half-light, move out to graze the lush grass of the meadows.

Massed conifers give the road between Wigglesworth and Tossie a spooky character at the "edge of dark", when the deer are at their most vocal. The Rev John Robinson, who became the minister of the old Tosside Chapel in 1860, had a strange experience concerning not deer but a big, black dog.

Mr Robinson had been to Settle. On leaving, to return home, he was followed by the huge dog, which refused to leave him. On passing through the tract of woodland which has now blossomed into a conifer forest, two men made as though to attack him. Immediately the dog sprang at them, quickly drove them off and stayed with him the rest of the way home.

Tosside Chapel, a magnificent survival of the type of religious building used by the old Independents, with balcony, high pulpit, harmonium and huge stove for heating the place, incorporates a Manse. It was here that the big black dog stayed overnight. Early next day, it moved off. The dog was never seen again.

The Golden Wyverns

Hellifield railway station is approached along Station Road in the village, which stands beside the A65. At the time of writing a new road has been made but not yet opened and the entry point is between Hellifield and Long Preston.

THIS IS NOT a ghost story but relates to a curiosity enjoyed by railway enthusiasts and also by small children, when invited to look for a winged dragon with a barbed tail and feet like those of an eagle which was set in the wrought-iron work on the island-station, built by the Midland Railway Company. When alarmed, the dragon sticks out a blood-red tongue.

It's not so much a dragon, despite what some local people believe, but a wyvern, now painted gold, which the Midland used as their emblem. Notice also the MR monograms. This station stands incongruously among the soft rounded hills of mid-Craven. The approach to the platforms is through a tiled subway which is so draughty it might be sub-let as a wind tunnel.

The Midland Railway took over running rights on the system north of Skipton and astonished their competitors by driving a railway up dale and through hill between Settle and Carlisle in order to have their share of the lucrative Scottish traffic. When Hellifield station was restored, iron roses on the canopy were painted in a contrasting red, to provide a contrast with the general whiteness of the canopy.

One of the strangest nights in the history of Hellifield railway station is recalled by Major Yorke, of Halton Place, when the Home Guard, raised during the 1939-45 war, was involved in what became known as the Battle of Hellifield. Col Clay, of Airton, was the commanding officer and Major Yorke was his adjutant.

A message was received from the police inspector at Settle asking them to call urgently, which they did. He produced a map which had been picked up on a bus in Burnley showing the whole of the Craven area right away up to Oughtershaw. Various farms were underlined with the words "Friends Here". The gist of it was that Hellifield station was to be taken over by an Irish army commanded by a German captain. The inspector wanted the Home Guard to muster a guard that night. He would quietly collect forty policemen.

The Home Guard had no arms except shotguns so it was

arranged that rifles would be provided by the Wakefield district and Major Yorke borrowed an old Sunbeam van from the Hellifield garage proprietor, who had been appointed transport officer. He went to Wakefield, collecting thirty rifles and about 200 rounds of ammunition.

It was arranged that the police would be moved into the railway station and the Home Guard would patrol the periphery, the password to be "Salmon".

Major Yorke had collected another thirty men, mostly Old Contemptibles, and encircled Hellifield station. When the rifles were unpacked, it was found they were covered with grease which had been smeared on them in 1918. Two policemen were seen walking down the line with revolvers, so someone shouted "Salmon. Salmon". The policemen jumped out of their skins on seeing two rifles levelled at their heads. Their alarm came from the fact that the police inspector had not told them the password.

When Major Yorke went to the village to report that the police did not have the password, he saw a policeman standing at the entrance to the subway, with one hand held up and another holding a pistol. Levelling a rifle at him was the Vicar of Gisburn, who was shouting: "Salmon. Salmon. Salmon!"

The Home Guard waited at their posts but nothing else of interest happened. Dawn came. The men were now getting bored. A gunshot was heard from the station. Everyone stood to and rattled the bolts of their rifles. Nothing else happened. It was reported that a man had pressed the trigger of his gun by mistake.

So the first phase of the Battle of Hellifield ended and the men fell out. The Home Guard were on special duty at the station for about a month. No one discovered if the map found on the bus in Burnley—a map marked "Friends here", "Withdraw to here" and "Irish friends here"—was genuine or the most wonderful hoax.

Chapel-le-Dale

Mahommet's Coffin

Chapel-le-Dale lies between two railway viaducts, at Ingleton and Ribblehead, and is traversed by the B6255. Weathercote Cave, which is roofless, is not open to the public.

THE REV JOHN HUTTON, of Kendal, one of the first gentlemen of taste and leisure who visited the Caves of the Ingleton district towards the end of the eighteenth century, was entranced by Weathercote. He descended into the abyss, passed under an arch of rock to see a waterfall 77 feet high, the water appearing from behind wedged boulder.

Hutton was a cultured man, well-versed in classical writings. He chanted verses from Virgil, Ovid, Addison and Milton during his tour. On the other hand, he may have looked up the references later and fitted them neatly into his text. Hutton, to whom Weathercote Cave was "the most surprising natural curiosity of the kind in the islands of Great Britain", called the perched boulder Mahomet's Coffin, comparing it to "the coffin of Mahomet at Medina". Hutton's *Tour to the Caves* was published with a list of local dialect words in 1781.

J M W Turner, the famous artist, stood in Weathercote Cave in 1808. Turner first set foot in Yorkshire in 1797, forming a close friendship with the Fawkes family of Farnley, in Wharfedale. The artist was eventually "discovered" by John

Ruskin and his work was nationally acclaimed. Ruskin was to write of Weathercote: "It is the rottenest, deadliest, loneliest, horriblest place I ever saw in my life."

Boggart of Hurtle Pot

You can look into Hurtle Pot from the lane which runs from St Leonard's Church to the farms at the foot of Whernside. The pothole is almost immediately behind the church. Be content to look from a distance. The great hole is muddy and there is a pool, complete with "black" trout.

THE COURTING couple who walked near Hurtle Pot, in Chapel-le-Dale, one evening, were local people who no doubt knew about the boggart, which was supposed to live at the bottom of the broad 58 feet gash in the limestone. They may have heard that this boggart had a habit of drowning people in the 20 ft pool. They were quite unprepared for the unearthly noises which suddenly arose from the tree-shaded pothole.

The two visitors fled in terror. Not long afterwards a man clambered from Hurtle Pot, and made his way back to Weathercote House, where he was staying with the Metcalfe family. He was carrying a flute and, like Orpheus, had been playing in the underworld. The tale was jotted down by a traveller named Walter White, mid-way through the nineteenth century.

White was told that "in olden times the boggart's deeds were terrible, but of late years he only frightens people with noises. Both this and Jingle Pot are choked with water from subterranean channels in flood time, and then there is heard such an intermittent throbbing, gurgling noise, accompanied by what seems dismal gaspings, that a timorous listener might easily believe the boggart was drowning his victims."

Priscilla Wakefield, a visitor in the early part of last century, described Hurtle Pot as "a most horrible, gloomy, deep, round hole, above thirty yards across at the mouth". She and her friends moved down a steep, slippery path to the edge of the pool at the bottom. Priscilla later noted that she nearly lost her life "from a deception of sight caused by the shining of the sun from above on the surface of the deep, black water, which, reflecting the lower part of the surrounding rocks, appeared like a rugged bottom just beneath."

She noted that swarms of large black trout lived in the subterranean pool, and one of them rose in sight as she was on the point of stepping, as she thought, on the shallow bed of rock, to catch it. The guide happily stopped her, "time enough to save me from inevitable destruction, for the water is of an unknown depth."

You had to be tough to be a tourist in the so-called Romantic Period.

Yordas Cave

This cave is on the left, near the head of Kingsdale, which is approached through Thornton-in-Lonsdale, near Ingleton. The road climbs, then enters this superb limestone dale, with grey scars on either side and a strip of cultivable land up the middle. The stream was canalised, hence its straight appearance. Yordas is not far short of Kingsdale Head Farm. The other farm in the valley is Braida Garth, and permission to visit Yordas should be sought from the farmer. The car is left at the road side. The approach to the cave is through a gate and up a short stretch of fellside. Torch and wellingtons ensure enjoyment in visiting a big limestone chamber with an ante-chamber known as The Chapter House.

YORDAS CAVE is said to have been named after one of the old gods of the Vikings, who most certainly colonised the area and set the basic pattern of sheep farming. The Vikings would know the cave, which had a mouth that really gaped until a landslip in the early part of the last century, though superstition may have kept them away.

Harry Speight, local historian, writing in 1895, said that Jordas (pronounced Yordas) was the Earth-god of the Norse sagas, from the word "earth". A poor woman, big with child, is said to have died when she sheltered in Yordas while on her way up the dale and over to Dent Town.

John Hutton, the aforementioned visitor during the later part of the eighteenth century, had his first glimpse of a cave at Yordas. He had hired a guide at Thornton-church-stile and the equipment included "candles, lanthorn, tinderbox, etc." The guide was a showman. He was enthusiastic about the sound caused by the discharge of a gun or piston. Fortunately for Hutton, no one had a gun.

The huge cave had been scarred and battered by vandals, some of whom not long before had defaced "both throne and chapter-house of their pendant petrified works, which had been some ages in forming."

John Houseman (1800) explored Yordas in the company of William Wilson, an old soldier, who was one of the guides to be hired at Ingleton. He was "a proper guide...furnished with the necessary apparatus of a lanthorn, long candlestick, &c., for the purpose." Wilson was familiar with the cave and respectful to those in his party. "An account of his own adventures fills up the vacant intervals of time."

He stood on a fragment of rock and struck up his lights, six or eight candles, put into as many holes of a stick. "With each, by the help of a long pole fixed therein, he could illuminate a considerable space...His tobacco-pipe, being prepared and lighted, is held in his mouth; with his flambeau in one hand and a staff on the other, the cock of his hat being placed before, he gives us the signal of a march."

The cave guide took a tumble. His "collection of luminaries, tumbled into a brook, had nearly left us in darkness, but when he fell we were more particularly afraid lest he should drop into some deep chasm of the rock, which might have proved fatal." (There is no danger of this in Yordas).

William Westall, the artist, visiting the area in July, 1817, drew the cave. A few days later, a waterspout burst on the fell and a torrent brought down great stones and masses of earth which half-filled the entrance to the cave.

Malhamdale

Behind the Cove

Approach Malham via Gargrave or Coniston Cold, which are on the A65 between Skipton and Settle. Then as you motor you will have a dramatic view of Malham Cove, a huge limestone cliff, in its setting of green pastures and futuristic pattern of grey walls. Another approach is from Settle, up the hill and across the moor, bearing left for Kirkby Malham. The road offers a view of the Cove and its setting from a higher angle.

WHAT LIES behind Malham Cove? Visitors over the years, who have seen a beck emerging from a letterbox-like slit at its base, have pondered on the subterranean world through which the water has flowed. Some have foretold that a huge cavern would be found there. What forms of life would exist in the perpetual darkness and peaty water?

Malham Cove, a natural limestone cliff with a slight bow shape, gives the dale a spectacular headpiece. A clergyman on holiday who visited the Cove in or about 1830 hired a guide. "While praying vows to the genius of this sequestered place, my guide at my direction struck up a tune on a clarinet. Music at such time, I think is in its place, and is most calculated either to soothe the broken spirit or enkindle the nobler passions of the mind..."

The visitor distinctly heard the music echo five times, when played "from a certain stone near the great cliff. It has a most pleasing effect on a fine summer's evening." The point at which the clergyman stood has been forgotten.

Another clergyman, the Rev Charlies L Tweedale, of Weston Vicarage, near Otley, became known as the Spooky Parson because he was forever communing with the spirits of the dead. He claimed in 1932 that he had a knowledge, gained from the spirit world of what lay behind the 240ft cliff. Tweedale handed to the chairman of the Parish Meeting an envelope, secured by five blobs of wax, which held a summary of his ideas. The seals were to be broken and the contents read when an underground system had been explored.

At that time, someone with the imagination of a Jules Verne might weave a fantasy about Malham Cove and create a subterranean world of caverns decked by stalactites, populated by people who live in perpetual darkness, nourished by albino fish. It would contrast with Charles Kingsley's chubby little water-babies, who frolicked in cool, clear Malham Beck.

The envelope was opened when cave-divers squeezed their way underground (Tweedale had suggested using dynamite to excavate an entrance tunnel) and explored a mile or so of an extensive system of caverns. It simply confirmed some of the ideas which Tabitha, one of the spirits, had revealed to the clergyman. There would be tunnels and submerged pools.

The divers, John Cordingley and Russell Carter, spending up to five hours in flooded passages, eventually broke through into a large passage, with some air bells or air-space chambers. The two men had worked in the system for years when the break-through occurred. Clearing a way through ten feet of boulders, Russell found himself looking into a black space. He was low on air, so John explored further. The gap turned out to be the entry into an apparently blind chamber, with no obvious way on. Then he saw a tiny slot on the left wall. It was a tighty squeeze, just big enough to get through.

John wriggled to the point where he thought he would be

stuck and have to back out. ''I looked up—and all I could see was blackness. We had popped out of the wall of the big passage, which we named Hel's Bells, after Hel, the Norse god of the underworld. The new passage, a key to further exploration, was named Aire River.''

The explorers continued their exploration and found, some 1,800ft from the entrance, a chamber they named Moon, the surname of the local farmer, who had been helpful. There may be another two miles of passages to explore. So far, no aquatic fairies or waterproof gnomes have been found.

Queen of the Fairies

From the car park at the National Park Centre, cross the road, seek out a footbridge, cross it and turn right to follow a well-made path for one and a-quarter miles to a mossy gorge, with a fan-shaped waterfall and a hole in the rock said to be the home of Jennet or Janet, Queen of the Fairies. Today, the waterfall, known as Janet's Foss, is owned by the National Trust.

IN 1792, the Hon John Byng, the man who was to become the fifth Viscount Torrington, travelled on horseback through northern England. He was impressed by the natural splendours at the head of Malhamdale. Byng and a local guide

visited Gordale Scar. He examined Janet's Foss, the fan-shaped waterfall in a mossy dell. The guide pointed out "a little, snug, dry cave", as Byng wrote in his diary. The guide said it was once inhabited by fairies but they were quite out of fashion. Byng, moved by the tradition, wrote six charming verses called *The Fairies Dance*. The poem began:

> *Little Gennet, Fairy trim*
> *To the merry Dance leads on*
> *Full of pastime, full of whim,*
> *With her playmate, Oberon!*

The blithe spirits of this area are the attractive birds—dipper and grey wagtail on the beck and a wren busy working over a mossy area for food. A rookery in the tree tops ensures that in spring and early summer the tract of woodland is never quiet.

A Ghostly Banquet

Kirkby Malham is the next village down the dale from Malham. The dale church, Minster of the Dales, stands here, and around it is a large churchyard. There is parking space at the church, though it would be kind not to use it at service times.

GO TO THE churchyard at Kirkby Malham at midnight and you may find that a banquet has been spread out for you by the Devil. The story of Malhamdale's "banquet of the dead" was first told in 1857 and was re-told by J H Dixon. Once you go to the banquet you will "go always and finally sup with the old gentleman in his abode of darkness". The Devil asked a boy named Kitchen and the Vicar (Rev Martin Knowles) to his banquet, which was laid out on a tombstone. The parson looked over the range of food and asked for salt. All the food and the Devil disappeared.

Nidderdale

Dead Man's Hill

The nearest most people come to the Hill, which lies between Nidderdale and Coverdale, is when they are following a popular footpath round the reservoirs of Angram and Scar House. Use this circuit to get the flavour of the area. The track beyond is a proper rambler's job, especially in winter. The reservoir access road begins with a well-signed right turn between Lofthouse and Middlesmoor, at the head of Nidderdale. Since 1975, the public has been permitted to use the road at a small charge. There is ample parking and also toilets. The hale and hearty might visit the reservoir area directly from Middlesmoor (where there is a small car park). The lane beyond the Park has the chilling name of Rain Stang.

THE NIDD and its upper tributaries gain strength on the eastern flank of Great Whernside, in an area where the landscape is remote and wild. Heather grows in the drier areas. Sphagnum gives a bilious green appearance to the mosses. Great slabs of peat, moist and brown, contain remnants of an ancient forest which they slowly throttled during a wet, peat-forming age.

On the high land, the melancholic double-note of the Pennine Whistler, as the golden plover was known, is a feature of spring and early summer. An eerie, goat-like bleating from the cold sky comes from a snipe which, while diving, extends the outer feathers of its tail. The air rushing between the bars makes the haunting sound, which chills the blood of a human visitor on days when the moors are covered by mist.

In this almost lost world stands Dead Man's Hill. The dead man was, of course, a pedlar. North country folklore has been enriched by the mysterious deaths of pedlars in wild places! If the pedlar actually existed (and there is no documentary evidence) he was probably a Scot on his way from Coverdale to Nidderdale by the shortest route.

Alfred J Brown, a great moorland tramper, wrote that before the water engineers had disturbed the source of the Nidd, the route was regularly used by Scottish pedlars who called at the isolated farms with their wares. He then related a story (told with variations of other remote inns) in which the blame for missing pedlars settled on an old woman and her son. They occupied a cottage-cum-resthouse near the hamlet of Woodale on the Nidderdale side of Dead Man's Hill. The cottage was often used by benighted travellers.

One pedlar who was capable of defending himself left the village of Horse House, in Coverdale, at dusk with the idea of spending a night at the cottage over the hill. He was shown to his bedroom. He ignored a bedside sleeping potion and snored loudly, lulling the old lady into believing he had gone into his last sleep. The old dame entered his room with a knife. Her son followed. Their guest watched every movement out of the corner of his eyes and while holding a dirk beneath the blankets. He leapt up, settled his account with the two villains in turn, and made the road safe for the Scottish pedlars who followed.

Brown also mentioned that Irish navvies working on two great dams at the head of Nidderdale had their own way of laying the dead man's ghost. They swarmed over Dead Man's Hill by a short track of their own making and got to the Thwaite Arms at Horse House. Then, re-crossing the hill again by moonlight, and with skinfuls of strong liquor, they were prepared to take on all-comers.

Guy Ragland Phillips, in his book called *Brigantia,* thought the name of the Hill might relate to some prehistoric human sacrifice. Harry Speight (1906) considered the Hill is probably the Nidderhow of a charter of 1250 which defined the boundaries of the Byland Abbey lands locally.

Wrote Speight: "It received its present appellation from the horrible circumstance of three human (headless) bodies having been discovered here in 1728 buried in the peat. They were supposed to be the remains of three Scotch pedlars who, after disposing of their goods, came to a foul end while traversing the lonely road out of Nidderdale into Coverdale. Yet some say they were murdered at one of the lonely farms in the dale, and that their heads were severed from the bodies to prevent identification."

Speight found a relevant record in a township book of Middlesmoor, under the date May 30th 1728: "Three murder'd Bodies were found burrd. on Lodge End without heads." The date of the crime was not known. No one concerned was ever brought before the magistrates. The bodies interred in Middlesmoor's consecrated ground were probably, as Guy Ragland Phillips suggested, from humans sacrificed in prehistory. The heads would have been ceremonially removed and buried elsewhere.

This moorland area is little-known, even among ramblers, though a popular track from Starbotton crosses to Kentucky, at the head of Walden, introducing a visitor to the austere countryside. Years ago, the farmer at Kentucky told me of a horse which died and was buried on the moor. During the 1939-45 war, some unused bombs were off-loaded by a German aircraft returning from a raid on the west coast. One of the bombs fell where the horse had been interred. Its bones were scattered far and wide.

A Roadside Grave

Greenhow Hill, between Grassington (Wharfedale) and
Pateley Bridge (Nidderdale) is served by a good road,
B6265, which attains an altitude of about 1,200ft above sea
level. A popular feature on the Grassington side are Stump
Cross Caverns, where a visitor can tour a cave system in
comfort and by electric light. The soldier was buried by the
road on the Nidderdale side of the Hill.

AT GREENHOW, farms and houses are thinly spread across
moors which bears the marks of lead-mining on the grand
scale. A skyline burial ground has a lych gate inviting you
(Biblical style) to lift up your eyes to the hills. At Greenhow,
you are invariably looking down on them.

John Kaye, a soldier, was buried at the roadside, where he
dropped from heat exhaustion while on a forced march. The
position of the grave passed from generation to generation of
Greenhow folk but in the 1880s some lead-miners thought it
was nobbut a tale. They decided to investigate and dug into
the ground. A spade clinked against bone, part of a skeleton,
with some brass buttons and (some say) even a gun to iden-
tify the soldier's remains.

The grave was marked with a headstone and, there being
a mine level immediately beneath it, by the shape of a coffin
carved into the roof of the mine. Whenever a miner passed
that spot, he would "give John Kaye a knock".

Miners at Greenhow

Inquire locally about tracks leading to the places where lead
was mined. Do not on any account venture underground.
The Museum at Pateley Bridge will repay a visit.

HARALD BRUFF, who had Norse blood in his veins, jotted
down much of the folklore of Greenhow and its people, but
for romantic tales of ghosts and superstitions, I turn to

97

Halliwell Sutcliffe and *The Striding Dales,* where he wrote: "These old lead-miners knew, too, when they were accused of superstition by folk who stayed above-ground, the mystery things that happen in the underworld..."

Sutcliffe was much moved by the bleak upland quality of Greenhow and that other work of the underground systems, caves and mine levels. He wrote: "A strange, desolate country, this of Greenhow, whose loneliness seems only deepened by the unsheltered road that winds through it, a narrow ribbon of grey."

The miners were not fanciful men, "yet once in a while they would speak of hidden matters. There was one who reached the mine-head before his fellows, and went down the ladders alone, impatient for his work. They came later on and found him dead in a narrow gallery, with queer marks about his throat. Well, poor lad, he should have known it was not good to go singly into any mine. The trolls fear numbers, but are wolves on the track of a lonely man. That was his comrades' summing up."

Sutcliffe himself was fanciful yet his book has endured through several editions into our brassy age. He wrote of the Ghostly Shift, when sounds were heard by miners underground which indicated another shift was arriving. The sounds stopped. There was no one to be found. "Men of Cornwall drifted to our northern highlands, following the lure of lead-mining. They brought with them the rich, Celtic gift of 'listening to the other world' and their spirit-lore mingled with the ancient, native beliefs handed down by Norse and British ancestors of ours."

Then there were the Knockers. Their loud tapping indicated to miners that they were approaching a rich mineral vein.

George Gill, who many years ago owned Stump Cross Caverns on Greenhow, made my blood run cold with his tales of ghostly sounds (usually of clogs-irons against stone) on moonlit nights. The implication was that t'Owd Man, though dead, refused to lie down.

He related how a member of a cave survey group was camping at Stump Cross one night when there was a full moon. He heard the sound of clogs coming down the road about midnight and he left his car to investigate. The sound came nearer, passed him and went towards Greenhow. There was no one to be seen.

In 1939, when George was living at Greenhow, he heard the sound of clogs outside the house. Once again, the moon was full. Clogs rang on the gravel of the road, then on the cobble stones by its side, and finally on the gritstone slab at the door. There was no one to be seen, either by George or his wife.

From another of t'owd 'uns on Greenhow, I heard of the time when ghostly clog sounds indicated that a man had just dismounted from a bike before walking beside it. A bystander looked in the direction of the sounds. There was no one about.

Weathered Rocks

Brimham Rocks are approached from the B6265 between Pateley Bridge and Ripon. The Rocks are owned by the National Trust and much information about them is available locally.

JENNY TWIGG and her Daughter Tib, isolated pillars on Fountains Moor, are seen by few. Not everyone has the stamina or inclination to walk for miles across dark moorland to see what William Grainge, in his book on Nidderdale, referred to as "tall upright pillars" which "at a distance have the appearance of gigantesses in broad bonnets".

Visitors by the thousand are recorded at Brimham Rocks, about which my old friend Guy Ragland Phillips commented: "These are probably the most impressive group of natural rocks in Britain...high, contorted, sometimes ludicrous, often terrible pillars like gigantic stalagmites without the cave to contain them...Between the dark rock pillars are deep, narrow chasms carpeted with green grass, brown heather and yellow sand...There are even big tunnels through the rocks which it takes some effort to resist and which have magical traditions attached to them akin to those of the wishing-wells."

Most of the rocks have names. If you put the middle finger of your right hand into a little hole in The Wishing Rock, and silently wish, then you will have good luck if not the realisation of your wish. The unsteady Boat Rocking Stone moves if touched by a honest man.

The Green Man

Fountains Abbey is a short distance from the small city of Ripon and is also to be approached from Ripley, near Harrogate, and from the Pateley Bridge road, B6265. Signs direct the motorist to a new visitor centre, from which it is but a short walk on a well-made track down to the ruins.

THE JEWEL in the crown of the National Trust properties in the Dales is set in the valley of the Skell near Ripon. In summer, it rises grey and majestic amid a thousand shades of green. That is the time when I visit the Green Man. He is not a small rotund figure with an antenna sticking out of his head who arrives by "flying saucer", as in the best space-age fiction. This Green Man, aged about five hundred years, is carved in stone and occupies a cramped position at the apex of a window in the Chapel of the Nine Altars.

He has a wild, some say evil, expression—not the sort of effigy one would expect to find at a Cistercian abbey which was dedicated to high thinking and simple living. The tradition he represents may hark back to Celtic paganism and to legends of small, secretive beings. In Ireland, they eventually became

Green Man at Fountains Abbey

leprechauns—"the little green people"—who doubtless had some cousins in Yorkshire.

Was the figure at Fountains carved to scare off evil spirits? He certainly scares me, with that wild look and with branches of a vine (or could it be oak?) growing from his mouth, framing his face with leaves.

A man who had more than a passing interest in the Green Man was Howard Strick, one time warden of Grantley Hall, who had a passion for the medieval period, introduced archery to Grantley and in his leisuretime enjoyed looking for traces of the Green Man. At Ripon, he found what he called The Green Batman. Long before an American devised a cartoon figure called Batman, a wood-carver at Ripon decorated a misericord, a hingled seat in the cathedral choir stall, with a figure that looks like a Green Man carved upside-down. The little face had, indeed, become that of a bat, hence the inversion. This Green Batman dates from the thirteenth century.

Howard told me that the Green Man image bobbed up in church decoration and documents (and also on some pub names) for at least eighteen centuries—and presumably originated in the "mists of antiquity" and a remote pagan past. The mysterious figure captured the imagination of the craftsmen who built and adorned the great churches and cathedrals. Early versions have a demonic aspect. Howard wondered if they were intended to shock sinners and send them scuttering back to the straight and narrow path.

The Green Man had his heyday when most of Britain was covered in forest so dense and vast that the superstious mind thought of it as being the haunt of strange beings. Even in these days, when most of us are urbanised and sophisticated, to be lost in a wood at nightfall would be a terrifying experience. Our lively minds would soon conjure up beings like the Green Man. He doubtles became the same character who, as Jack in the Green, took part in medieval ceremonial, wearing a custume which covered him with leaves. He was the mischievous fool or jester who danced ahead of the procession.

Guy Ragland Phillips referred me to the writings of John Richard Walbran, a Yorkshire historian early last century, who imagined the Green Man's head was entwined with serpents, not with branches, and concluded the head represented the principle of Evil, or more probably of Pride. Walbran's guide ran to twelve editions, by which time all devilish or pagan associations of the head at Fountains had been discreetly removed.

Fountains Abbey ghosts have been filmed, in monochrome and colour, when the abbey is floodlit, but the effects may be simply tricks of the light. One photographer recorded what were taken to be the faces of a monk and a girl on a pillar.

When Fountains Hall was built, stones from the Cistercian

abbey were re-cycled. The hall, completed in 1611, is a remarkably fine example of a Jacobean dwelling. The daughter of Sir Stephen Vyner was "cruelly done to death" and it may have been her ghost which was seen in the building where she became known as the Blue Lady.

A Moorland Temple

The Druid Temple is situated on the moors between Healey and Ilton. It may be approached from Lofthouse in Nidderdale, using a high road which descends to run beside Leighton Reservoir. Some little way beyond the outflow of the reservoir look for an Ilton sign (right) and then Jervaulx Forest, a new creation, where there is a car park, picnic area and a good track leading a short distance to where the "temple", once open to all the winds, now has a forest setting. An alternative approach is westwards from the market town of Masham, skirting Swinton on its way to Ilton. Its location is marked on most tourist maps.

THIS STRANGE assortment of upended stones—a North Country Stonehenge—was built early last century and when the Forestry Commission bought the land they planted what is known as Druid's Plantation. The Druids would not have known it. They made no use of stone structures. I have visited the temple many times. On an autumn day, when the trees drip water and mist swirls between the trees, it is indeed a spooky place.

The building of this moorland temple is attributed to William Danby, born in 1752 at the family seat, Swinton Hall, and in descent from a family who acquired the lordship of Masham during the reign of Henry VIII. Danby dissipated much money and energy in rebuilding Swinton. The poet Southey, who visited him here in 1829, described this landowner as "the most interesting person whom I saw during this expedition, a man of very great fortune and now very old." Danby had played a notable part in Yorkshire life, being High Sheriff in 1784.

Why did he create the strange hilltop temple? It was constructed in the 1820s, which was a time of considerable local unemployment. He provided work for men whose income had been lost and at the same time gratified his urge to build something distinctive. It is thought that the designer was Robert Lugar, an architect who specialised in castellated Gothic and who worked on Swinton Hall from 1821 until 1824. Perhaps the temple was the obligatory ruin or folly for the estate at a time when Gothic was fashionable. A man engaged in the work of temple-building was paid at the rate of a shilling a day.

It was said to be a replica of Druidical Circles, based on those in Co. Sligo, Ireland, and in Anglesey. It is not a true circle, being oval in shape, with a length of about seventy-five feet by fifty feet wide. The axis lies in a north-south line. The tallest of the stones is ten feet. Two large flat slabs are thought to represent the altar stones. I have seen some human visitors being "sacrificed" for the benefit of visitors' cameras. In a cave at one end of the temple is luminous moss, Schiso-stega, or Elfin Gold.

The temple has had a woodland setting for many years. One tract was clear-felled in 1916. The Forestry Commission planted the present block of conifers, which obscure several other stoneworks related to the Temple. These consist of trilithoned (three-stoned) outposts on which tylers were placed as watchmen during a service. It is fun looking under the tree canopy, trying to locate them. They are mysterious in their gloomy, mossy setting.

It is still possible to walk from the temple to the lip of the ridge and gaze across Leighton Reservoir and the calluna moors around Nidderdale.